CW00921536

The
Redundancy
Survival Guide

The Redundancy
Survival Guide

Assess your legal rights, explore career options
and turn redundancy into opportunity

Rebecca Corfield
Barry Cushway

KOGAN
PAGE

First published in Great Britain in 2010 by Kogan Page Limited

Kogan Page Limited
120 Pentonville Road
London N1 9JN
United Kingdom
www.koganpage.com

© Rebecca Corfield and Barry Cushway, 2010

ISBN   978 0 7494 5761 7
E-ISBN 978 0 7494 5949 9

British Library Cataloguing in Publication Data

A CIP record for this book is available from the British Library.

Typeset by JS Typesetting Ltd, Porthcawl, Mid Glamorgan
Printed and bound in Great Britain by MPG Books Ltd, Bodmin, Cornwall

Contents

Introduction

About this book

This book has been written to cover all aspects of redundancy. It includes what happens when an employer decides to make redundancies, your attitude and reaction to that event, and what comes next for you in terms of your future career.

You may just have heard that you are to be made redundant or have opted for voluntary redundancy, or the prospect of being laid off could just be a general worry for you at work. You may be aware that redundancy could be a possibility and feel that you want to arm yourself with a clearer picture of what you could and should do if it happens.

There are lots of negatives about redundancy: financial difficulties, anxiety about supporting yourself or your family, the prospect of mounting debt, worries about hardship and losing your lifestyle, lack of confidence, self-doubt and the fear of being in a job market of shrinking opportunities.

For many people though, redundancy offers a real opportunity to find a better job than the one they left. That forced change can lead you to discover things about yourself and find resources that you did not even know you had. It can be used as a time to take stock. Are you really doing what you want to do with your life?

This book will help you to clarify your particular redundancy situation so that you can make the most of every opportunity. From knowing the legal picture to guiding you through negotiating your financial package, it shows you how to maintain a confident manner as you plan for the future. This involves thinking through all the options and developing your choices so that you can achieve career success.

The authors are experts in employment law, human resources, job-search techniques and career coaching. Both have also been made redundant themselves in the past.

How to use this book

You may want to read this book through completely if you need to feel more in control of the whole process of being made redundant and what to do next. For some readers, it will be more useful as a tool to use to dip into at different points in their experience of redundancy.

Throughout the book you will find practical exercises and checklists to prompt you in your thinking about your career and your preparations for the next steps you will take. Scattered in the text you will see tips labelled 'Take action!' These are specially picked pieces of advice to get you started. Real-life questions appear in different chapters. Reading the answers may prove useful to some of your queries too. You will also find 'Key points' at the end of each chapter that sum up the main aspects to remember from it. Whatever your next move, this is the start of the next phase of your life.

The meaning of redundancy

The significance of redundancy

While there may be 50 ways to leave your lover there are only six ways in which you can legally be sacked or, in the usual jargon, have your employment terminated. These are:

■ misconduct;

■ capability – ie inability to carry out the job to the required standard;

■ redundancy;

■ where continuing to work would break the law in some way, eg if someone employed as a driver lost his or her licence;

■ retirement;

■ some other substantial reason not covered in the above categories.

The key heading we are concerned with is redundancy. If you have lost your job or are in danger of doing so it is important to be clear about the reason, because losing your job through redundancy brings with it a number of rights and does not carry the stigma of some of the other reasons for termination. In fact losing a job because of redundancy should really be regarded as an opportunity. Personal experience indicates that redundancy can lead to new opportunities, to discovering resources you did not know you had and perhaps finding more satisfying employment or self-employment. Moreover, this will be underpinned by a tax-free payment from your last employer.

Legal definition

The common legal definition of redundancy originated in the Redundancy Payments Act 1965 and is now contained in section 139 of the Employment Rights Act 1996. This states that an employee is dismissed because of redundancy if the dismissal is wholly or mainly attributable to:

(a) the fact that his employer has ceased, or intends to cease

    (i) to carry on the business for the purposes of which the employee was employed by him, or

    (ii) to carry on that business in the place where the employee was so employed, or

(b)   the fact that the requirements of that business –

(i)   for employees to carry out work of a particular kind, or

(ii)   for employees to carry out work of a particular kind in the place where the employee was employed by the employer have ceased or diminished or are expected to cease or diminish.

To decide whether or not you are in a situation that involves redundancy, it is necessary to consider the various elements of this definition.

Conditions applying to redundancy

You need to be an employee

Although it may seem obvious, not everybody who works for a company is an employee of that company – agency staff for example. However, if you have a written contract of employment then the answer is straightforward and you would be entitled to all legal rights applicable to any employee being made redundant.

Your employment should have been or be likely to be ended by the employer

You can only claim redundancy rights if your employment is ended by your employer. If you voluntarily resign you would generally lose any right to claim that you were made redundant. It was your choice to leave. The situation is the same if you leave 'by mutual agreement'. Of course any good employer who feels that redundancies may be unavoidable might ask for volunteers. In such a case, although by volunteering you are actually resigning there is normally an incentive offered, such as an enhanced redundancy payment in addition to your normal legal rights, to encourage you to do so.

Should you volunteer to be made redundant?

Where an employer does ask for volunteers there are usually conditions attached to this request. Prime among these is that the employer will usually reserve the right not to agree to some requests as doing so might deprive the company of people with essential skills or experience. You could find yourself in a situation where although you would like to leave on redundancy terms you are not allowed to do so. This can be difficult for both parties.

It can happen that when you know that redundancy is a possibility you start looking round for other opportunities, and if you have found such an opportunity it can then be frustrating to realize that you might have to resign without the prize of a (potentially tax-free) redundancy payout. This is naturally demotivating and relationships can become strained. The temptation in this situation is to try to work your ticket by being awkward enough to make the employer let you go. However, this is a dubious course to pursue and you could end up losing your job on grounds of conduct or performance if you push matters too far. There is no point in souring relationships if you can avoid it as you never know when this could come back to haunt you, and you may need a reference. There is a saying in the theatre that you should always be nice to people you meet on your way up as you may meet those same people again on your way down.

What if the employer tries to make you resign?

The reverse position is when the employer wants you to leave, for whatever reason, but may be reluctant to end your employment for fear of ending up in an employment tribunal or perhaps to avoid making redundancy payments. In these circumstances the employer may be tempted to put pressure on you to resign, for example by giving you some of the less desirable jobs, by leaving you out of meetings, by reducing your bonus payments or by worsening your working conditions. However, most employers these days are aware that if they push things too far and you are forced to resign they could end up facing a claim for constructive dismissal (see Chapter 5). This occurs when you resign because you feel that the employer has behaved so unreasonably that you are left with no other choice.

In reality this is not much of threat, because to bring such a claim you would first have to resign and then you would have to bring a case against the employer and win it. Even so, few employers will push matters so far that they might end up facing such a claim. They can, however, still make life difficult but if you do end up resigning you solve their problem. The rule therefore is never to resign but leave it to the employer to make a reasonable offer.

Can the employer change your working hours or pay as an alternative to redundancy?

Perhaps a more common scenario that could also potentially lead to a claim for constructive dismissal is where the employer is not actually trying to lose staff but rather is seeking a reduction in working hours or pay to enable the organization to cope with a loss of income or profits. If you voluntarily agree to such changes there is no problem, but if the employer unilaterally imposes such changes on you this is likely to be a fundamental breach of the contract of employment and potentially constructive dismissal if you resign as a result.

Have you actually been dismissed?

There are also circumstances in which it may not be clear that you have been dismissed. For example if, in a fit of pique the manager says 'Get out of here, I'm sick of the sight of you' or words to that effect, does that amount to a dismissal? It is in fact most unlikely that an incident of that kind would be treated as a dismissal, and if it were it would almost certainly be an unfair one. For a dismissal to be effective there would normally need to be some written notification of it, as most employees are entitled to a written statement of the reason for dismissal. You can of course be dismissed without any such written notification and if, for example, the employer just stopped paying your salary or wages, that would be a strong indication that the employment had ended.

If you are working on a fixed-term contract with a definite expiry date and that contract is not renewed by the employer, that also amounts to a dismissal. Whether or not you would be entitled to a redundancy payment would depend on how long the contract was for and how long you had been working continuously for that employer.

The employer could decide to require you to do a different job. If a change of role is suggested to you and you agree to it, then there is no issue. If, however, the employer arbitrarily changes your job without your agreement, then you have in effect been dismissed from your previous job and could be entitled to a redundancy payment.

The requirement for the work you are employed to do must have ceased or diminished at that location

Where is your normal place of work?

Your normal place of work is a key consideration. If the organization has closed down or the business has ceased trading or is in the process of doing so, then the matter is relatively clear-cut as all locations will close and any employees will be redundant as a result of the closure. Similarly, if the organization continues in existence at other locations but is being closed at the place you are employed, that is also a relatively clear-cut redundancy.

The place you are employed at should be set out in your statement of employment particulars, which all employers must provide. Although there may be mobility provisions (requiring you to work in other locations from time to time) in the statement or elsewhere in your employment contract (the contract is not usually just one document but can include any offer or other letters, staff handbook, written and verbal agreements etc), what counts for the purpose of determining redundancy is your normal place of work.

If you have only ever worked at one location there should be no problem in concluding that this is your place of work. There can be complications, however, if you have been required to work at several different locations, but generally the employment contract should be able to clarify the position. Whether or not redundancy applies depends on the wording of any mobility provisions, but generally it is likely that a change of location will give rise to a potential redundancy claim.

What if the company remains open at your workplace but requires fewer staff?

The position is less straightforward where work has not ceased but has diminished. A reduction in work may mean that the employer does not now need to employ the same number of people. There is no particular rule quantifying how much this reduction needs to be and it is for the employer to decide how many and what type of employees are needed to achieve the company's business objectives. In fact there does not need to have been a loss of business; the employer can just decide to reorganize the work in such a way that fewer staff are now required to achieve the same output. The application of new technology and changes to systems and procedures can have this effect.

There are also a number of examples of companies that have had to reorganize work during a temporary absence, such as sickness, only to find that they could manage perfectly well without the absent job holders. Being away sick during a period in which redundancies are being contemplated can of course add to an absentee's anxiety.

If the employer tells you that your job is not required and makes you redundant but then immediately appoints someone else to do broadly similar work, even if the job title is different, then this is unlikely to be a genuine redundancy and you might have a claim for unfair dismissal. This does not mean that the employer cannot take on other staff doing different jobs or in a different location, or indeed increase the size of the workforce if there is a sudden upsurge in business, such as winning a new contract.

The employer could also appoint someone to do your job but still make you redundant provided there is an overall loss of jobs within the organization. The employer is allowed to shuffle the pack in this way.

Takeovers and mergers

Takeovers, mergers and changes in ownership can lead to redundancies. Generally, when there is a change of this kind, the majority of staff will transfer to the new organization and retain their existing terms and conditions of employment. Employees not offered jobs in the new organization will technically be redundant.

Anticipated reductions in business

Finally you should note that redundancy also applies where staff reductions are considered necessary because of an anticipated downturn in the requirement for that work, not just where it has already happened. However, the expectation of such a downturn has to be more than a vague feeling that less output will be required and has to be based on a clear projection that fewer employees will be required. It has to be more significant than a normal fluctuation in levels of demand. Most employers are unlikely to want to go through this kind of process unless there is a relatively strong conviction that it is absolutely necessary.

Work of a particular kind

The definition of redundancy states that it occurs when the requirement for 'work of a particular kind has ceased or diminished'. In essence this means that if the employer's requirement for the work you have been engaged to do, or are actually doing, has reduced or disappeared then your job is redundant. This is a matter for the employer to judge.

Changes in the type of work

The employer has the right to reorganize work to suit the needs of the organization and this includes changing duties and responsibilities, so if you are asked to take on different or additional tasks this will not normally be a redundancy. If the job changed out of all recognition and was completely different from the one you were appointed to do, then if you refused to take on the new role and management insisted, this could lead to a dismissal (for which there could be various reasons), but unless the requirement for the work you had been doing had 'ceased or diminished' it would not be a redundancy. Presumably the work would still be required but would be carried out in a different way or by someone else.

Key points

1.   For your job to be redundant the requirement for the type of work you do must have ceased or reduced at the location where you are employed.

2.   For redundancy to apply you must be an employee of that organization.

3.   Your employment must have been ended by the employer (not by you resigning).

4.   If the employer changes your job or reorganizes work, this does not amount to redundancy.

2

Your redundancy rights

When you are about to be made, or have been made redundant, there are a number of rights that apply to you. These rights are either legal rights or contractual rights. Legal rights are part of the law of the land whereas contractual rights may not necessarily be written into the law but are contained within your contract of employment. The legal rights establish your minimum entitlements but your contract might add to or improve these. The legal rights that apply to you include:

- the right to be consulted;
- the right to be accompanied at certain meetings (this may not be a strict legal right but it could be a contractual right);
- the right to be offered suitable alternative employment and to a trial period;

- the right to notice;

- the right to time off to look for work or undergo training (provided you have two years' service);

- the right to redundancy pay (provided you have two years' service);

- the right not to be selected for redundancy for unfair reasons;

- the right not to be selected for redundancy on grounds of maternity or pregnancy.

Each of these rights is considered in turn in the sections below.

The right to be consulted

You are entitled to be consulted in advance about any proposed redundancy. This means that you should be told:

- that a redundancy or redundancies are possible;

- the likely numbers of redundancies;

- when these are likely to occur;

- the reasons for the redundancies;

- why your job has been selected.

The employer has an obligation to consult you even if no final decision has yet been taken about redundancies that are being considered.

If 20 or more redundancies are being considered, the employer also has an obligation to consult any trades unions or employee representatives to discuss ways of:

▓ avoiding redundancies;

▓ reducing the number of planned dismissals;

▓ mitigating the consequences of dismissal.

This consultation has to be genuine, not just the employer going through the motions, and the overriding aim should be to reach agreement. In situations like this it is an advantage to belong to a trade union that can represent your interests.

The consultation meeting

To carry out this consultation the employer has to arrange a meeting with you and should notify you of this in writing. The purpose of the consultation meeting is to alert you to the possibility that your job may be at risk of redundancy and to give you time to consider your options. For example, you may wish to suggest to the employer that instead of being made redundant you might be prepared to work shorter hours or – between gritted teeth – take a pay cut. Neither prospect is that appealing but they may be options that you prefer to a permanent loss of your job.

Equally you may be happy to accept redundancy subject to certain conditions or guarantees. For example, some people might be happy to leave an organization with a suitable compensation package because it affords an opportunity to become self-employed, and if they can negotiate some guarantee of consultancy work with the former employer it gets them off to a good start.

How long should the consultation period be?

Although there are minimum consultation periods set out for collective redundancies (eg at least 30 days where more than

20 but fewer than 99 employees are being made redundant) there is no prescribed period where fewer than 20 workers are affected nor for consulting individuals. However, the length of the consultation period should be reasonable.

What is reasonable in your particular organization is likely to depend on the size of that organization and what may be contained within your employment contract. Really it is up to you to say how long you need to consider the position and the employer ought to be prepared to give you between two and four weeks if necessary, although in reality you are likely to require somewhat less.

At this initial meeting no final decisions should have been made by the employer, otherwise it is not a genuine consultation. The conversation should indicate that your job might be at risk but if the employer says 'We are going to make you redundant' or words to that effect, it sounds as though his or her mind is already made up, in which case the consultation meeting is just a charade. Any redundancy dismissal that leaves out this stage, or just goes through the motions without having any serious intention to listen to any points raised through the consultation process, is likely to be unfair.

What happens after the consultation meeting?

Following the consultation meeting there should be a further meeting at which you will be able to make any points that have occurred to you following the consultation meeting. If the redundancy is confirmed at this meeting then you are effectively being given notice of termination of employment. You should normally be given the further right of appeal against this decision.

The omission by the employer of any one of these stages could potentially make a redundancy termination unfair. Whether or not it is actually unfair depends on the circumstances, and it is difficult to be entirely prescriptive about this.

The point, however, is that the employer has to treat you fairly and has to follow any organization redundancy procedure. From your viewpoint, the employer's failure to follow this kind of process gives you a basis for complaint that can be used as a negotiating lever.

The right to be accompanied

The law states that you have the right to be accompanied by a colleague or a trade union representative at any disciplinary or grievance meeting that could result in action being taken against you. Although the law is not clear about whether this includes being made redundant, most employers interpret it in this way. Even if this is not an absolute legal right it may be the case that the organization's procedure provides for this, making it a contractual right.

This does not mean that you have the right to be accompanied at a consultation meeting, because this meeting should only be to discuss the possibility of redundancy, any other options that might be available and to discuss the kinds of issues set out above. No action should result from this meeting as it is only exploratory. This does stop you from asking to be accompanied, and some employers' procedures do provide for employees to be accompanied at all stages, including the consultation meeting.

If you have any form of disability, for example one which might make it more difficult for you to communicate, it would be unreasonable for the employer not to allow a companion who could help in this respect.

Who should accompany you?

The legal right to be accompanied only includes the right to be accompanied by a colleague or a trade union representative,

not a friend, relative or solicitor. If you want to bring someone else the organization is within its rights not to allow
this. Some organizations, however, do allow a 'companion'
without defining this term, in which case you could bring
along someone else, such as a friend or relative. You need to
be careful about this however, as whoever accompanies you
should not damage relationships (see Chapter 4).

Most people elect to be accompanied by a colleague and
this usually presents no problem, but if the employer feels that
the person selected might be disruptive you could be asked
to select someone else. Again bearing in mind that the ideal
outcome is a negotiated settlement, it would be wise to choose
someone who would be likely to be mutually acceptable. It is
up to you to get that person to agree to this role. Some may
be reluctant to take part for fear that it might damage their
position in the organization.

Another option is to be accompanied by a trade union representative. This can apply even if the organization does not
have any recognized trade unions. If you have personal membership of a trade union then they will be able to provide
representation and you will have the comfort of knowing that
there is a trained representative there to support you. Of course
it does mean joining a union and paying the subscriptions,
and you would have to consider how much need you might
have for their services in the future.

The extent of involvement of the companion is for you to
agree between you but usually the role would include:

- acting as a witness;

- putting your case;

- summing up your case;

- responding to any views expressed;

- keeping notes of the meeting.

The companion does not have any right to respond to questions on your behalf.

The right to be offered suitable alternative employment (and to a trial period)

The employer has a duty to consider what suitable alternative work might be available. If you are offered an alternative position within the organization, this must be similar to your previous role and appropriate to your level of knowledge, skills and experience. It would be inappropriate, for example, for a sales director to be offered a permanent job as a call centre operator or a receptionist. Similarly the job should be appropriate in terms of the level or status of the job and the remuneration package. Work is likely to be regarded as unsuitable if it entails significant changes to:

- pay;
- working hours;
- travelling time;
- skills;
- status.

Any offer of alternative employment must:

- be made before the old contract terminates;
- enable you to start work not more than four weeks after the ending of the old contract;
- be the same as or not substantially different from the old job and suitable for you.

What if you are offered a job at a different location?

The offer of alternative employment should also be at the same location; that is, the one that is set out in the statement of employment particulars that forms part of your contract of employment (if you do not have one of these you have a potential claim against the employer). You can turn down an offer of alternative employment at a different location unless your contract includes 'mobility provisions' that can require you to work at different locations within the organization. Whether any offer by the employer is reasonable depends on the alternative location suggested and the wording of your contract.

Does accepting an alternative job affect the right to redundancy pay?

You can take on a completely different job within the organization, but it has to be your choice.

If you are offered but reject suitable alternative employment you are likely to forfeit any right to redundancy pay. Similarly if you do not respond to any such offer this is likely to be seen as an unreasonable refusal, with the same consequences. If you do accept a new role you have a period of four calendar weeks in which to try out the new job without jeopardizing your right to a redundancy payment if the job proves unsuitable. However, to retain this right you would need to give notice before the end of the four weeks. This period can be extended by agreement with the employer if you do not feel that four weeks is long enough to give the job a fair trial.

The employer must give you enough information about the proposed job to enable you to make an informed decision about it. This should include details such as pay, hours, status and location.

The right to notice

Notice periods

If you are dismissed for any reason (apart from gross misconduct – see below), not just redundancy, you are entitled to be given a notice period. This means that you remain an employee of the organization until the end of that notice period and you only leave when it expires.

How long this notice period lasts depends on a number of things. In most cases the notice you are entitled to will be that set out in the employment contract. For most monthly-paid jobs this tends to be a month. However, there are also legally prescribed minimum notice periods, based on your length of service, which employers must give you. Experience suggests that employers are not always aware of these so you could find yourself in the position of needing to remind them. These legally prescribed minimum notice periods are shown in the table below.

Period of continuous employment	Notice entitlement
Up to one month	None
One month to two years	One week
2–11 years	One week for each year of service
More than 12 years	12 weeks

Whether it is the notice period in your contract or the statutory period that applies depends on which is more favourable. So, for example, if you have five years' service you are entitled to five weeks' notice, even if your contract only entitles you to four weeks'. Equally, if you have 15 years' service you would be entitled to 12 weeks' notice. On the other hand, if your contract entitles you to three months' notice but your entitlement through length of service would be less than this, it would be the contractual period that would apply.

The only situation in which an employee would not be entitled to notice is if dismissed for gross misconduct, which is the commission of such a serious offence that the employer is justified in sacking the employee on the spot. This includes such things as violent conduct, theft and drunkenness but clearly cannot apply where the reason for dismissal is redundancy. Even if you are on a fixed-term contract you should be given notice that the contract will not be renewed at the end of the term.

If you are not given the proper notice period and you take the matter to an employment tribunal, then the tribunal will work out what notice you should have been given. This is particularly significant where the addition of the notice period brings your length of service to over two years because this brings with it additional entitlements.

Notice means paid notice, so you should receive your normal salary during the notice period. You should also keep all your normal employment benefits for the notice period. For example, if you are given a company car you should be allowed to retain this until the end of the notice period, although there is nothing to stop you negotiating to have the value of the benefit rather than the benefit itself.

As you remain an employee of the organization it also means that you have to work normally and continue to give your loyalty to the organization. While it can sometimes be hard to remain loyal to an organization that appears not to value your services, being negative or disruptive can backfire, especially if you are dependent on the organization for a good reference or you work in a sector or a job where there may be close links between different organizations in the same industry. Word can sometimes get round quickly and there are companies that specialize in collecting data about potential candidates, including compiling blacklists.

Garden leave

Frequently when staff are made redundant the employer would prefer those affected to leave the organization straight away rather than remain as a possible source of discontent or disruption. Many are understandably concerned about possible misuse of data. For this reason redundant staff are often told that they do not need to work during the notice period. You may sometimes find that there is what is called a 'garden leave' clause in your employment contract. This simply states that in certain circumstances the organization can require you not to come to the office nor to take part in normal organization activities. If this appears in your contract then it is likely that the organization has the right to tell you that you do not need to work during your notice period. This is obviously good news because it means that you can take the notice period as time off while still getting paid for it.

If there is no garden leave clause in the contract the employer could still ask you not to work the notice period. Again this is good news, because why would you want to? However, if you wanted to be awkward you could insist on working, as the employer has an obligation (although not normally written in the contract) to provide you with work and by failing to do so is technically in breach of the employment contract. However, it is difficult to see any real practical advantage in insisting on working when you do not have to. Perhaps one situation in which this might be of value is where the notice period is a long one and there is a danger that you might get rusty or lose touch with the latest developments.

There may also be circumstances in which you consider it a good idea to work your notice period so that you can accumulate commercial data, such as contact details of customers or clients, that may be of value to you in your next employment, or in setting up your own business. You should be wary of doing this as most companies where this might be an issue usually incorporate a non-competition clause in the employment contract. This would look something like the following example:

> For the protection of the Company, its business, its employees, and its customer base, you agree that:
>
> you shall not, during the six-month period starting with the date of termination of your employment, either on your own account or with or on behalf of any other person, solicit or entice away or try to solicit or entice away from the Company, any individual who is an employee of the Company;
>
> you shall not, during the six-month period after the date of termination of your employment, either on your own account or with or on behalf of any other person solicit or entice away or attempt to solicit or entice away, any Company customer; and
>
> you shall not, during the six-month period after the date of termination of your employment, either on your own account or on behalf of any other person, have dealings, directly or indirectly, with any Company customer. However, you are not prohibited by any of these restrictions from seeking or doing business with a Company customer which is not in direct or indirect competition with the business of the Company.
>
> You agree that these restrictions are reasonable and necessary for the protection of the Company and that if any of these are found by any Court to go beyond what is reasonable to protect the Company's interests that the remainder of the contract will still apply as modified.

Although these types of clause may not always be completely enforceable in the courts, which are reluctant to agree to anything that might stop a person from earning a living, if the organization for which you worked was able to prove that it had suffered a loss as a result of your actions then you could be held liable.

Pay in lieu of notice

As stated earlier you are entitled to be paid your normal wage or salary during the notice period. However, the employer can ask you to leave immediately and to accept pay in lieu of notice. This is not quite the same as garden leave, during which you remain employed and receive your normal pay.

By asking you to go without being able to work your notice period, the employer is technically in breach of the employment contract by not allowing you to work when you have the right to do so. The good news is that in this case any payment to you is actually damages paid by the employer for defaulting on the contract, so is likely to be free of any tax and NI deductions.

Be warned however, that if there is a clause in your contract stating that the employer reserves the right to give pay in lieu of notice, this gives the employer the contractual right to pay you instead of giving notice, and this then becomes normal remuneration which is subject to the usual statutory deductions.

If you are paid in lieu of notice then your employment ends on the date you are notified and you can go and work for someone else straight away.

The right to time off to look for work or undergo training

When you have been made redundant you have the right to paid time off to look for work. This includes not only going to interviews but also other time spent finding employment such as attendance at a job centre or employment agency. The law does not specify how much time off you should be given but tribunal cases have indicated that up to two days per week might be reasonable. You are only entitled to this time off if you have had two years' continuous employment with this employer, by the end of your notice period.

The time off to undergo training can include training for a completely different kind of work. It does not have to be related to the type of work you are currently doing. You can have time off for both job-seeking and training, and the fact that you have had time off for one aspect does not mean that this should be set off against the other.

The right only applies if you have been given notice that you are being dismissed because of redundancy, and it only applies during the notice period.

Time off is limited to your working hours, that is, those set out in your contract of employment. There is no right to any time off if you are paid in lieu of notice.

Pay during time off

You are entitled to be paid for this time-off absence at the appropriate hourly rate. Where your working hours differ from week to week your pay should be calculated by taking the average over a period of 12 weeks, ending with the last complete week before the day on which the notice was given.

If the employer unreasonably refuses to pay you for this time off you can make a claim to an employment tribunal, but any award against the employer would be subject to a maximum of two-fifths of a week's pay. Any complaint of this kind has to be presented within the period of three months beginning with the day on which it is alleged that time off should have been allowed, although this may be extended by the tribunal if it considers that it was not reasonably practicable to present the complaint within the three-month period.

The employer has the right to ask you to provide evidence of the reason for the time off, so you should keep records of any letters or e-mails inviting you to appointments.

The right to redundancy pay

Basic entitlement

If you have two years' continuous employment with your employer then you will be entitled to redundancy pay. There is a legal maximum compulsory figure that may be taken into account when calculating this amount.

What this means in practical terms is that if you are paid £300 per week then that is the figure the employer would have to take into account when calculating your redundancy pay as it is below the statutory maximum figure. If, however, you are paid say, £400 per week, the employer only has to base the calculation on the lower statutory maximum figure of £380.

Calculating redundancy pay

Basically, the payment is calculated by multiplying your years of service by your weekly pay, subject to the statutory compulsory maximum. However, this calculation is slightly complicated by the fact that there is an adjustment to the figure depending on your age at the time of being made redundant.

For service between the ages of 22 and 41, the calculation is a straightforward one of one week for each year of service. However, for service between the ages of 18 and 22 it is only half a week's pay, while for service between the ages of 41–61 it is one and half a week's pay for each year of service. For persons aged over 61 the figure is the same as for a 61-year-old.

Fortunately the Department for Business, Innovation and Skills produces a useful table for calculating entitlement and this is reproduced as Appendix 1. To use this simply read across from your age at the date of redundancy shown in the left-hand column and down from your years of service at that date shown across the top of the table. For example, someone who is 45 years old with 10 years' service would be entitled to 12 weeks' redundancy pay. Further information is available from their website www.berr.gov.uk.

Enhanced redundancy payments

The figures set out in the above paragraphs are the amounts the employer is legally obliged to pay, provided you have the required two years' service. However, the employer can also at his discretion pay more than this and many do so. The usual ways in which redundancy payments may be enhanced are by:

- ignoring the cap on weekly pay so that the redundancy pay calculation is based on what you actually earn not just on the £380 per week figure (which is clearly of no benefit if you earn less than this);

- multiplying the earnings figure by more than the 0.5, 1 or 1.5 weeks recommended;

- a combination of the two above options, by taking actual earnings (if above £380 per week) and multiplying these by a higher figure.

There are a number of other payments to which you are also entitled if made redundant. These include payment for:

- salary during the notice period or pay in lieu of notice;
- any holiday not taken;
- the value of any benefits during the notice period.

You should also check your employment contract and staff handbook to see if there are any clauses relating to severance payments on being made redundant. Many larger organizations have negotiated redundancy and severance policies that may be more generous than the statutory payments and it is these that would apply to you. It is also the case that if the organization has previously made other employees redundant, the terms applying in those cases might also apply to you. This is not necessarily the case as those staff might have been in a different employment category (for example terms applying to company directors are often different from those applying to other employees) or might have been subject to a one-off settlement. However, if the employer has previously applied a particular policy or approach on a regular basis, it could have become part of your contractual entitlement through custom and practice.

Ex gratia payments

Employers can also, at their discretion, make what is usually described as an *ex gratia* payment. This is simply an additional amount paid to compensate you for 'loss of office', sometimes described as a 'golden parachute', although the latter will usually only apply to very senior jobs. Any *ex gratia* payment is typically free of tax up to £30,000. Such payments, especially for senior executives, might take the form of cash, benefits or shares. They are, however, only a right if incorporated into the employment contract. Such payments are considered further in Chapter 4.

The employer is required to give you a written statement setting out how the redundancy payment has been calculated.

What happens if the organization is insolvent

If the organization goes broke then, provided you satisfy the qualifying conditions, you will still get any redundancy payments you are entitled to because the Department for Business, Innovation and Skills maintains a fund specifically for the payment of redundancy pay in these circumstances. However, you would only get the basic statutory entitlement.

The right not to be selected for redundancy for unfair reasons

Unfair selection criteria

There is a long list of selection criteria that if used would be found to be automatically unfair. These include:

- Union membership: you cannot legally be made redundant just because you are or are not a union member or because you refuse to join a union.

- Legal industrial action: you cannot legally be made redundant because you are participating in or have participated in legally sanctioned industrial action. Broadly speaking, this is industrial action following a legitimate ballot.

- Because of your activities or carrying out duties as an employee representative.

- Because you took action in relation to certain health and safety matters.

▓ Because you asserted a statutory right such as the national minimum wage or the right to request flexible working.

▓ Because you took maternity, paternity or adoption leave, or for any other grounds related to maternity.

▓ Any reason relating to discrimination such as sex, race, disability, age, religion or belief, sexual orientation etc.

There are a number of other inadmissible reasons and a complete list of these can be found on the BIS website: www. bis.gov.uk.

The right not to be selected for redundancy on grounds of maternity or pregnancy

If you happen to be pregnant or are on maternity leave it is very difficult for the employer to make you redundant, unless the whole company, office, outlet, factory or similar unit is being made redundant as well. If there are any jobs available you should be offered one of these, in preference to anyone else if necessary.

The reason for this is that if you are selected for redundancy by the employer it would be presumed by any employment tribunal to be because you are pregnant or on maternity leave and in practice it would be very difficult for the employer to prove that this was not the case. Any dismissal for pregnancy or maternity amounts to sex discrimination and would not only be held to be unfair but could also result in the employer having to make a significant compensation payment. In discrimination cases there is no limit to the amount of compensation that can be paid and employers are aware of this. In this situation you hold all the cards.

While this obviously offers good protection to one employee category it is not such good news if you are the other person to be selected in their place, which is not uncommon in small companies. If you do find yourself in this position there is not a great deal you can do about it as the employer clearly has little choice.

Employment references

The employer is not obliged to provide you with a reference, unless you work for an organization governed by the rules of the Financial Services Authority. Any reference the employer does give has to be fair and accurate. If it is defamatory to you or might otherwise prevent you from getting another job you could have a claim against the company, but you would need to get legal advice about this.

You do not have an automatic right to see any reference given by your employer, but under the provisions of the Data Protection Act you can ask a new or prospective employer to show you any reference given by your former employer. They might decline this request but if you took the matter to an employment tribunal there is a good possibility that it would find in your favour. Employers are generally aware that there is the possibility that any reference written by them about you might be seen by you at some time in the future.

Key points

1. You have both legal rights contained in the law of the land and contractual rights given by your employment contract.

2. You have legal rights to be consulted about redundancy, to be given paid notice and to be offered suitable alternative employment that you can try out for a period.

3. Provided you have at least two years' service you have a legal right to redundancy pay and to paid time off to look for another job or to retrain.

4. The employer should allow you to be accompanied at any meeting that might result in your redundancy.

5. Any offer of alternative employment must be appropriate to your skills, experience, employment status and circumstances.

6. You have a right to paid notice, which will be better than that provided in your employment contract or your statutory entitlement, which increases with length of service (up to a maximum of 12 weeks after 12 years).

7. You may not be required to work your notice period and may be given pay in lieu of notice.

8. Selection for redundancy must be based on fair and objective criteria and there are a number of inadmissible reasons.

9. Selection for redundancy if you are pregnant or on maternity leave could be direct sex discrimination.

10. Your employer is not obliged to provide you with a reference and any reference given should be fair.

3

Assessing your position

In this chapter we look at what has happened, the effect on you and how you feel about it. An important aspect of dealing with redundancy successfully is understanding the economics behind any layoff.

Even if you saw it coming, handling the rejection can be a major event to deal with. We will look at how you can think through and reinterpret the situation. If you are not happy about the position you find yourself in, you will need to deal with the difficult feelings that may follow. You need to find ways of facing your new reality so that you can take control and move forward.

What has happened?

Something major has occurred. You have been asked to leave your employment. It may have been coming for some time and you may have been glad to take the redundancy offer, or it may have been a shock announcement that took you by surprise. Even if you knew that there were going to be redundancies in the organization, you may not have dreamed that your name would be on the list.

There may have only been a couple of people to be laid off or it may be the whole of the workforce. This may mean that the company will be able to carry on operating with a smaller number of employees or it might be that they have stopped trading completely. The bigger the numbers involved, the less personally you may feel the loss of your job, but the more flooded the local labour market may be if you are all looking for similar work.

Unless you volunteered to take redundancy, perhaps because you were near to retirement age anyway or you wanted a change of career direction, you will have found yourself to be a passive recipient of someone else's decision. This lack of control is the element that can be difficult to handle. Other previous aspects of your career have been down to your choice – what career to follow, which jobs to apply for, whether to take a job and whether to stay with it or leave. This time someone else is calling the shots and you have had no choice in the matter. This was a compulsory redundancy.

Understanding the economics

Most redundancies are a reaction to, and a reflection of, prevailing economic conditions. If it has been handled properly, the reasons for choosing the candidates for the redundancy programme will be a mixture of external circumstances and picking the most suitable people. Your employer needed to reduce the costs of the business or wanted to reorganize the way that the organization was run. The people picked could be in particular jobs where the demand for services has fallen off or where the need for their role had diminished, or they could be a mixture of individuals in different roles as described in the last two chapters.

The financial situation out there in the real world is subject to change. The impact of a negative change is that companies need to downsize to survive, or sometimes they are affected so severely that they need to shut down completely. People need to be selected for these redundancies according to the criteria that have been decided upon. All these factors are relevant before any names are chosen. It is only at the end of the process that individuals are considered for redundancy.

This means that it has not been a personal choice against you, but is much more likely to be a combination of how long you have been with the company, what specific role you are in and how well different parts of the business are bearing up. You may be told how the decision was arrived at, or if not you may want to find out for your own information. Sometimes the best people are the ones to be laid off, perhaps just because they were brought in most recently.

Redundancies can be seen as part of the normal business cycle. Most organizations need to adjust the way they are organized periodically just to stay competitive and efficient. It could be that this wave of redundancies could be the only way for your company to survive as an economic entity.

Handling rejection

Even considering all the above you can still feel quite sore after you have been selected for redundancy. The plain fact is that you are not wanted any more in that job and your services are no longer required. You have been dismissed. It is worth reading that sentence again just to let it sink in. In some ways it does not even matter how the decision was arrived at – what is important is that it has occurred. As soon as the decision has been taken, your employment prospects there are nil.

Feeling rejected is very common, whether or not you wanted this redundancy to happen. It is a rational response to the fact of losing your job. Work takes up a large part of our lives and we invest it with an emotional significance in terms of it being a source of community and status. You can feel a strong sense of loss of identity and of your world being upended. It is a shock.

In this sense redundancy can be similar to other causes of emotional trauma such as marriage break-up, bereavement or illness. It can be helpful to realize how common these feelings are and that feeling all or some of them is completely natural and normal. It is only if particular feelings remain over time and don't progress into something more positive that you may need help.

Losing your job affects all the other parts of your life. It can feel embarrassing to talk about your situation to friends and family. The first question we often ask a stranger on meeting – 'What do you do?' – is suddenly awkward to handle. You can feel that the status that came with your job title or employer has vanished along with the employment. That can leave a big hole in your life even if you are comfortable with the change. It can also have serious financial implications as your regular income stream of wages or salary dries up forthwith.

Reframing the situation

Experience often only begins to make sense when we tell other people about it and get the chance to 'see' the situation for ourselves by hearing about it and getting some feedback. But how do you relate the story of what has happened without sounding like a total victim? To deal with it you may need to reframe or re-describe what has happened before you can tell the new story.

The position you were in was redundant and that is why you had to go. In other words, the fact that you were in that particular job at that particular time is why you have been made redundant. If you had not been in that job at this time, it would not have affected you. This fundamental truth is the antidote to keep in your mind all the time when you may be feeling a failure. It just happened to you at this time and has no bearing on your future employment prospects.

Practise using a neutral tone at least when you talk about this news with people. If you get into a discussion about it, try consciously to pick out the positive points of what has happened to you. You may not be aware of them but there could be lots of advantages in the longer term.

Positive aspects of redundancy could include:

■ New horizons may open up.

■ Different options may become apparent.

■ You may be getting out of a dying industry/struggling sector.

■ Leaving the old job may be a chance for a more positive future.

■ You may be leaving with a pay-off before the firm collapses.

- There is a chance to retrain.

- It is a time to rethink your future.

- You can evaluate where you are in life.

- You can make new choices and proactively pursue a career.

- You can choose the subsequent step instead of just drifting into the next thing to come along.

- You may enter a different social scene.

- There could be more opportunities.

- You can change your work–life balance.

- There is time to take a break and have a breather.

- It could be a time for a holiday.

This is an impressive list and I am sure that you could find that some of these items apply to your case. This is not just a way of diminishing the fact that you have been laid off, but is a useful technique for acting in a more positive fashion. If you can make yourself conscious of the advantages, it will help to keep the difficulties in proportion.

Athletes and performers use this tool when they are about to compete or perform. If you visualize the best that can happen to you and talk up the situation to highlight the greatest expectations you could have and the winning outcome you would like to experience, you are more likely to live up to your own publicity. Your attitude and reactions can be affected by the way you yourself approach the problem. In the sporting world, if you believe you can win, you will have the winner's swagger, you will walk tall and have an easy smile on your face. Your tone will be confident and your voice strong and clear. You could just convince the opposing competitors that you have the match all set up, even before it starts.

Take action!

Work on running through the list of positive aspects of redundancy often in your mind to keep your worries in perspective.

Dealing with depression

Whilst we have just been talking up the potential benefits of redundancies, in some cases, events can take a more serious turn. Feeling down after a job loss is a well-known syndrome. Being out of work can feel very lonely. You are the only person at home when everyone else is at work. No one can understand how it feels to be unwanted and the feelings of worthlessness can migrate to the other aspects of your life.

It is quite natural to feel displaced and despondent about the fact that everything is going to have to change. These feelings can move to feeling useless and worthless. In extreme cases people can be driven to any of these:

- difficulty in sleeping;
- alcoholism;
- loss of sex drive;
- feelings of violence;
- thoughts of suicide.

All of these can result in a long period of not being able to cope. If you start to feel like this, you must get help from a doctor because several of these symptoms together could mean that you are starting to feel depressed. Depression is an illness. A GP can help you to deal with these symptoms with medication that will not be habit-forming, for long enough for you to start to get better. Your doctor can also help with other types of therapy if they are needed.

Emotional pressure can emerge in a bodily form to make us feel physically bad or ill. Mind and body are more connected that we realize. With redundancy, you have suffered a loss and that needs to be acknowledged and recognized in order to deal with it. The more you can indulge yourself to uplift your feelings, the more upbeat you will feel in other ways too.

Helping yourself to feel better can be encouraged by simple things that give you pleasure or relax you. Music can be energizing or restorative, so use it to enhance the positive feelings you are looking for and keep the dismal, downbeat songs for another day. Similarly, exercise releases endorphins, which are chemicals that enhance positive feelings. Join the gym, take a daily walk or just boost the amount of regular exercise you get to keep you feeling alive and healthy.

An allied response to stressful situations is apathy. That feeling that everything is just a little too difficult to overcome; the lack of initiative to get to grips with things; the resulting passing of the days, turning into weeks, then months with no change in your circumstances. The increase in feelings of despair and hopelessness as this situation becomes the norm can lead to real difficulties as nothing is being handled or organized.

No one gets a new job just dropped in their lap. You need to go out and get it. If you are stuck in a rut you need to break it by adding new and useful habits into your life. Start with the easy bit – reintroduce routine into your life then slowly add in more challenging tasks to take you forward. Take a look at this list to inspire you:

Health

Get up and go to bed at the same reasonable time each day.
Ban sleeping in the daytime.
Go for a short walk each morning wearing trainers.
Eat at normal meal times and not in between.
Cut out cigarettes completely and coffee after midday.
Cut right back on alcohol and eat more fruit and vegetables.
Visit the local health centre or gym for free classes.

Personal

Take a quick shower or bath every day.
Have your hair cut every two months.
Dress as if you were going to work.
Go to a free museum, concert or art gallery each month.
Do one housekeeping task each day.
Grow some plants – indoors or outdoors – or do some gardening.
Start a daily diary.

Social

Phone or write to one person each weekend just to ask how they are.
Take up some kind of study – improve your language skills or start to learn a new one.
Explore volunteering opportunities.
Join a Job Club through the Jobcentre Plus network.
Register with a new job-search site each week.
Borrow a book from the library to update your IT skills.

Take action!

Watch comedy shows and funny films. Laughing is good for you.

Facing reality

You have to deal with the position in which you find yourself. You need to move to acceptance of your situation so that you can move on. Your life has altered and you need to acknowledge and face this to progress to the next steps. What was your present employer is to become your last. What was a future period in which to find a new position or to move on to the next job has become the challenge of the present time.

One way of getting more objective about what is happening is to keep a diary, or log, of events and feelings. Any big stationery store sells week-to-a-view diaries that give about six short lines to write each day. If you describe events and also put down how you are feeling about life, you will be left with a record of what has happened and the story of your reactions to it. A real book is better than just doing it on a computer as the very writing of the entry each day is a creative task in itself.

You can take this exercise as far as you want. Some diaries can become more like scrapbooks to include pictures, tickets, photos and mementoes or other physical accessories as testament to the story you are relating. Although it may not be an activity you have tried before, keeping a diary can be a really helpful activity for lots of different reasons. Here are just a few of them:

- provides a record of events;
- puts the details down that would otherwise be forgotten;
- leaves an archive that remains as the time passes;
- gives a brief daily period for pausing and thinking;
- encourages self-reflection;
- allows events and feelings to be revisited and analysed;

- is a gateway to self-reliance;

- is something for you to organize in an otherwise out-of-control period;

- gets feelings out without needing them to be said;

- allows for self-pity, anger and other strong emotions to be safely expressed;

- acts as a pressure valve for bitterness and depression;

- enhances anything positive as it can be highlighted;

- enables understanding about how things are moving on;

- provides a resource to look back on for similar future experiences.

Some might say that this is a self-indulgent exercise but it can be an empowering way of moving through a difficult period of any kind. This is particularly true if you are a person who finds talking about your emotions difficult or uncomfortable; it can be a neutral way of letting go of feelings without getting bogged down in them.

Some people are perfectly happy about their redundancy situation. Others take longer to bounce back. But bounce back you must. Being out of a job is not the end of everything. There are a lot of worse situations in the world. You will look back at this stage of your life in the future and find it hard to remember exactly what happened. It feels significant now but you are already moving on to the next stage.

Taking control

So you are getting ready to find and plan a way forward. You will need to finalize your severance package, if you have not already done so, as your final act with your last employer. This is covered in the next chapter. Remember in all your dealings with them that you will be grateful for a character reference from them, possibly for years to come, so keep relations with your last boss constructive at all times.

To counter the fact that you have been out of control, you can increase the areas over which you have more influence. Explicitly set up things that are in your power. Your immediate environment can be full of the things that you want around you – from aromas, to music, to the people who give you energy and ideas. Spend time with friends and family with whom you don't need to keep explaining yourself.

This could be the perfect time to start a labour-intensive project at home. Getting your house in order can be a good thing to do after redundancy. All those home improvements and decorating tasks that you put off for ages might rise to the top of the agenda right now. Taking the initiative in non-work areas can make you feel proactive and motivated, just the antidote you need when other aspects of your life are out of your control.

Be aware too, though, that redundancy can affect other people as well as yourself. Those close to you may have worries about how you are, about the financial situation or about what is happening to your career. They may not feel able to talk to you about these issues, or they may try and then find it causes problems between you. Friends may not know how to initiate conversation that does not revolve around work and can feel awkward being with you as a result. People close to you may feel cross and disappointed about how the redundancy occurred. They may feel that by being angry on your behalf, it will make you feel better, not realizing that this reaction may not help you move on at all.

If you can be open and positive about what has happened and your journey through it, you will find this helps the people around you to react in the same way. So it will be down to you to take the lead on this. Although you may feel in need of reassurance yourself, this may be just the time that you are called upon to help other people to feel upbeat and motivated. Keep all lines of communication open so that you don't feel cut off and people close to you don't feel shut out and excluded.

Write a new script

From today on, a new story will be written by you to talk about your life and where it is going. From now on, you are in charge and you can determine how you and other people see your situation. You need to think about how you are depicting yourself to the rest of the world. Are you a passive recipient with a dismal outlook who has just had bad news, or do you see yourself as a person with options who is going places?

Look at these two different ways of talking about the same situation:

Just been made redundant	It's a good time to leave current job
Laid off	Have left
Thrown out	Decided to move on
Dismissed	Making some changes
No job there for me	There is a better opportunity coming

You are setting the tone, line and image now of what you have left, where you have got to and why. Everyone you talk to will take from you the picture of the situation. You can have them pity you and feel sorry for you, or you can intrigue them and interest them in your next steps.

Questions and answers

Q. I feel embarrassed that I have been made redundant and don't like admitting it. Are you sure that I won't be branded unemployable in other people's eyes?

A. Everyone is aware of the fact that redundancies are an economic response to a more challenging employment situation. Being made redundant is much more common and is better understood. For instance, both authors of this book have been made redundant in the past. This means that employers know that skilled and able people will lose their jobs in this way sometimes, often through no fault of their own.

Q. Several people locally were laid off at the same time. None were particular friends of mine but I wondered if it would be a good idea to get together with them as we all start to look for jobs?

A. It would definitely be a good idea to get together to combat those feelings of isolation. As long as you don't all just sit in the pub together, it can be a real boost to get a group going to support each other. Just being in the same situation means that you can take an interest in each other's position, keep levels of motivation up and compare notes. Get in touch with them soon and suggest a get-together.

Key points

1. Don't underestimate the significance of this event.

2. This has not happened for any particular personal reason.

3. It is important that you keep communicating with family and friends.

4. Work out how you are going to portray this situation.

5. The more you take control of those aspects that you can, the better you will feel.

4

Negotiating a severance package

Your legal rights when faced with redundancy are set out in Chapter 2. This chapter deals with how to negotiate payments and benefits above the legal minimum.

Understanding your negotiating position

The employer's viewpoint

Firstly, it is worth remembering that most employers do not usually want to be in the position of having to lay staff off. They are likely to be feeling uncomfortable with the position they find themselves in and may be experiencing a degree of guilt. You may have worked with each other for a long time, with the employer having some continuing feelings of loyalty to you. This gives you a degree of emotional leverage in the negotiating stakes. Also remember that employers are concerned about maintaining their good name. If you consider that you are being treated unfairly, you could even consider an approach to the press, although this should be regarded as a weapon of last resort.

Another option you could try is to approach other influential people within the organization. In some circumstances there can be disagreement about who should be made redundant. If you have supporters at the right level within the organization you may be able to persuade them to intervene on your behalf. Ultimately, if you feel you have been treated unfairly you could always raise a formal grievance through the organization's grievance procedure.

It is also worth bearing in mind that there are likely to be others in the organization who will be looking to see how fairly the organization treats you, especially if they feel they might be next in the firing line. Any perception of unfair or unreasonable treatment could undermine their morale and possibly make them think about their own futures and the employer is likely to be aware of this.

Finally and crucially, employment law is complex and no employer wants to face the prospect of being taken to an employment tribunal. Not only is the process time-consuming and potentially very costly, but it can also generate bad publicity for the organization. Even if employers have a strong case they are likely to be aware that tribunal cases can last several days and if solicitors and barristers are appointed this can be very expensive. For most employers it can also be a nerve-racking experience that they would much rather avoid.

If employers are aware that they may not have followed the correct procedure in some respect, for example by not adequately consulting you in advance of any redundancy, then they will be particularly nervous about the possibility of a tribunal claim so will be all the more keen to reach some kind of settlement with you.

You should also remember that, especially if you are in a senior position, you might have information about the organization that it might wish to be kept confidential. The employer would not unduly wish to alienate you if there was any possibility of this entering the public domain.

How to negotiate

Preparation

Ensure that you collect copies of any paperwork relating to redundancy selection procedures, including any staff handbook and also your own employment contract. Your position will also be considerably strengthened if you are able to find aspects of the process that might operate to your disadvantage before you find yourself selected for redundancy. If the selection criteria include a productivity measure that might have been affected by your sickness absence, for example, you should point out straight away that this would have an adverse effect on you.

If you work in an organization that has unions ensure that your union is involved in the process. They should be fully aware of all the issues involved. Even if the organization does not recognize unions there could be some advantage in you joining one to get the benefit of their advice. If you are reluctant to join a union you should still be able to get advice from any professional body you might belong to or from other bodies such as Citizens Advice Bureaux.

Monitor how effectively the organization applies its procedures. If it makes mistakes in the process, this could strengthen your bargaining position. For example, a failure to negotiate with employee representatives when making 20 or more employees redundant could result in compensation of up to three months' salary for each employee.

The initial consultation meeting

As set out in Chapter 2, you should be invited to an initial consultation and then to a further meeting. You should be given notice of this initial meeting in writing, and although there is no legal right to be accompanied at this meeting there is no reason why you could not ask to be. At this meeting, however, you should just listen to what the employer has to say but not give any immediate reaction. Of course such a meeting can come as a shock but you gain nothing by reacting negatively, or for that matter positively, at this stage. You should just listen to what is said and then consider the matter during the consultation period you should be given. There are a number of questions that could be asked at this time but it is probably better just to listen to what is said, give the issues some thought and ask your questions at the next meeting or during the consultation period between the two meetings.

The employer should offer you at least one week to consider the issue but you can agree to a shorter period if you think this is all you need.

The second meeting

The second meeting is the one at which you find out whether the redundancy is confirmed or not. If you are just told outright at the first meeting that your job is definitely going to be made redundant, then it is clearly not genuine consultation and the employer is already in breach of the correct procedure, a fact you can use to your advantage when negotiating.

Being accompanied by a colleague or trade union representative

At this second meeting you should ensure that you are accompanied by a colleague or a trade union representative. The right to be accompanied is described in Chapter 2. That person is there to act as a witness to anything said, which could be very useful not only to confirm any promises made or guarantees given by the employer but also in the event of any case being brought by you against the employer.

The presence of a third party means that the employer will be reluctant to bring any pressure on you to accept terms you are not happy with. On the other hand of course, the employer might be prepared to make you an offer that is more favourable than he or she is prepared to make to others, and the presence of a third party, who also happens to be an employee, could inhibit this.

Where you are accompanied by a colleague that person will have to continue working with the employer, unless of course he or she is also a candidate for redundancy. In such cases the employers will know exactly who they are dealing with and their likely strengths and weaknesses. This will not usually be the case with a trade union officer, except where the union is recognized by the organization when the person concerned is likely to be known to the organization's management.

Being accompanied by someone else

If you want to be accompanied by someone other than a colleague or a trade union officer but the procedures do not allow this, it may still be worth asking if you can do so, as many employers may not be familiar with the strict letter of the law and feel that by refusing such a request they are being unreasonable. If you have a disability that means that you cannot communicate clearly, for example, then it may be entirely valid for you to be accompanied by someone who can help with this. Your employer is required to make reasonable adjustments in relation to disability and this may well fall under that heading.

Being accompanied by a relative

Generally it is not a good idea to be accompanied by a close relative as they are likely to be too emotionally involved in the issue. You should try to keep the discussion as reasonably calm, professional and amicable as possible in the circumstances. Nothing will be achieved by being confrontational and an aggressive attitude might make employers dig their heels in and be less receptive to any suggestions you might make.

Of course you may decide that you want to keep any discussions, or the fact that you may be made redundant, to yourself and so elect not to be accompanied. However, this does mean that you would not have a witness to anything that might be agreed or to check your understanding or recollection of what was said during the meeting.

Questions you may want to ask

There are a number of questions that you might want to ask at or prior to this meeting. These will not only give you vital information to help you in your negotiations but will also make it clear to the employer that you understand the issues and are not someone who can be taken advantage of. Some of these questions are discussed below.

What are the reasons for the redundancy?

The reason for asking this question is to satisfy yourself that it is a genuine redundancy and not just a pretext for ending your employment for some other reason. The employer's response will usually be along the lines that the requirement for the kind of work you are doing has ceased or reduced, or that the organization generally has suffered a decline in business and savings have to be made by reducing staff numbers.

If your job is the only one of its kind and there clearly has been a reduction or a loss of the need for your specific services, the position is relatively straightforward as it is your job that is redundant. However, if the reason is that there has been a general decline in demand affecting the whole organization, or a significant part of it, and your job has been selected for redundancy in preference to others, there are a number of additional questions you should ask, as set out below.

Who else has been selected for redundancy?

If you are one of a group of staff all performing the same or similar roles, for example as sales representatives, you need to know whether it is just your job that is at risk or whether all the jobs in that group are equally affected. If it is just your job, you need to find out why you have been singled out.

If it includes all jobs of that type then it is likely to be because the demand for the services provided by those jobs has reduced or disappeared, but you need to have this confirmed by the management. If only some of that group of staff are affected, again you need to know the reason for those selected being included within the redundancy pool. This leads to the next question.

What criteria have been used to identify the jobs to be made redundant?

Employers often have difficulty in deciding the right criteria for selecting those staff to be made redundant as employment law presents many pitfalls for them, especially if the basis of the selection is discriminatory. For, example, in one case in 2007 a park worker dismissed on redundancy grounds by Lambeth Serviceteam Limited won a compensation payout of £550,000. This was because the employer had failed to consult employees adequately about the redundancies and had used selection criteria, including absence levels and the ability to drive a car, which were seen to discriminate against disabled staff. It was assumed that the person who won the award would not work again. Of course now he does not need to.

Last in, first out (LIFO)

A favourite basis for redundancy selection used to be what was known as LIFO – last in, first out. In other words, the prime candidates for redundancy were those who were most recently appointed. While this could be viewed as rewarding loyalty and those with long service, it could be discriminatory on grounds of age as more recently appointed staff are often likely to be younger. A recent court case suggests that using length of service as a basis for selection is probably acceptable but there remains an element of doubt, so it is an approach that you could legitimately question if it suits your purpose to do so.

First in, first out (FIFO)

The converse of this was FIFO – first in, first out – which again used to be a common approach. In past years many employers went through a phase of choosing redundancies from those aged over 50, later realizing that in the process they had lost far too much experience. Such an approach would now clearly fall foul of the age discrimination legislation.

If either of these approaches is applied to you, there is a good chance it could be used as a basis for disputing the validity of the redundancy.

Legitimate selection criteria

So what selection criteria can the employer legitimately use? The employer can take account of the skills, qualifications and aptitudes required by the organization now and in the future. There is no one prescribed way of conducting such an audit, or indeed the content of it. It could relate to just skills and experience, for example, but it could also include attendance and disciplinary records, when it really becomes more than just a skills audit. Equally, there are no rules about how the various skills elements should be weighted or scored or about who should conduct the audit. Some organizations employ an external body to carry out this role, but while this has the merit of objectivity the external auditors can only go by the information they are provided with, including past appraisals and other written records.

Skills audits

If you are faced with the prospect of a skills audit you need to get chapter and verse about exactly what is to be included, how the various elements are to be scored and who is to conduct the process. Where there are employee representatives it will usually be their role to get clarity about these issues. Once you are clear about the criteria to be assessed you should not hesitate to seek advice, for example from any professional body or trade union you are a member of, about completing any form or undergoing tests as part of the process.

Occupational tests

Any tests that are applied should be relevant to the job you were doing or may be required to do. If, for example, you are tested or assessed on report writing skills but you are not required to write reports, this would probably not be a fair criterion. However, if the organization intended to change jobs so that this became a part of the requirement of those jobs and this was a legitimate change, then such a test is likely to be reasonable.

Equally, as the case described earlier illustrates, if you have a disability and the required skills or tests were designed in a way that made it more difficult to meet the necessary standards, then they are likely to amount to disability discrimination, rendering any dismissal based on them unfair.

If you have a disability but are required to take tests, it is up to the employer to provide all necessary facilities and arrangements to ensure that you can compete on an equal footing with everyone else. If you are from a particular ethnic or cultural background, the tests should be designed to take this into account and should not be more difficult for you in relation to your colleagues just because of your background.

While a skills audit could legitimately include aptitude tests, especially for skills-based roles, there is no reason why it could not also include other types of psychometric tests such as those designed to identify personality traits, behavioural competencies or team fit. The main problem with these is that they are not precise measures and it is a very subjective judgement to decide that an organization requires certain types of personality characteristics. The use of tests of this kind in this context should certainly be questioned.

There are also a range of tests designed to measure intelligence or thinking skills, and although the use of these is less common these days they do at least have the advantage that you can revise for them, up to a point. There are many books on the market giving information about how to pass various types of test, and research has shown that practice can improve performance in these. You cannot really practise answering personality questionnaires because you do not know what the tester is looking for.

Job performance
The employer can take performance into account. However, for this to be a valid criterion the employer will need to have

clear performance records. While this may be relatively easy to measure and provide evidence for in the case of such hard measures as sales generated, items checked, invoices processed, it is much more difficult to both measure and demonstrate performance levels for jobs with much less tangible outputs such as those that form the core of most managerial, professional and administrative jobs. If performance is cited as the basis for selecting your job, ask for the evidence in support of this.

If your performance has not been to the standard required there should be evidence of this from past appraisals and warnings. You should have been clearly told what it is that you were not doing to the required standard, have been given a chance to improve, told what would happen if you did not improve and been given any necessary training to help you reach that standard.

If you have not had an appraisal for a long time, you could argue that your performance has since improved. If the employer places too much emphasis on performance, it could imply that the real reason for selecting you is not because your job is redundant but because it may be easier for the employer to terminate employment on the grounds of redundancy rather than pursue a long-winded termination on the grounds of capability. It obviously takes a lot longer to terminate employment on the latter grounds as the employer has to build in time to give additional training and then to assess whether there has been any improvement.

There may also be faults with the appraisal process itself. One of the biggest problems with any appraisal scheme is that most, and in some cases all, of the performance measures depend on the subjective views of managers. It is difficult to get consistency between managers, and while one person might think that all his or her staff are superstars another might regard the same group as being below the required standard. These kinds of variation in judgement are likely to be greater where there is no second-tier vetting or review by another person in the organization. You may be able to argue that the appraisal scheme results are flawed for this reason.

Of course if you do feel that your performance has not been up to scratch, and this can happen for many reasons not always under your control, then it may well suit you to leave on redundancy grounds as this does not carry the stigma of a dismissal for poor performance.

Where performance is used as a redundancy criterion the employer must also take into account the effect of any disabilities on performance. He or she must also make allowances for the impact of absences such as maternity or paternity leave. For example a decision based on sales performance that might have been affected by this type of absence during the reference period would be likely to be unfair.

Performance standards

When we refer to performance this usually relates to the level required to do a job to a fully satisfactory standard: the 100 per cent level. However, there is no reason why in a redundancy context this should not relate to the relative standard of performance; that is, comparing your performance with those of people carrying out similar jobs. Even though you could be meeting all required targets and generally satisfying the criteria for fully acceptable performance, if you are nevertheless not achieving the same levels as your colleagues it would be legitimate to single you out for that reason.

If you find yourself in a situation in which you may be made redundant on the basis of performance criteria, you need to ask the employer to set out the precise criteria and to explain how you do not meet these. If the basis is your performance appraisals, you may be able to argue that these are not valid for one of the reasons suggested above.

If you are dissatisfied with any explanation given or do not feel that you have been given sufficient information, you should seek clarification and ultimately, if this does not satisfy you, the issue could be taken further through the organization's grievance procedure. It is fair to say, though, that if matters have reached this stage you should probably be considering alternative employment anyway.

Conduct and attendance records

The employer can take your previous conduct and attendance record into account as a basis for selecting you for redundancy. If an employee has a string of disciplinary warnings, perhaps coupled with a poor attendance record, this would clearly make that person a prime candidate for redundancy under these criteria. As with the performance criterion, however, the employer has to be able to provide evidence in support of such decisions and is subject to the danger that this might be seen as an excuse for terminating the employment of a troublesome employee and not a genuine redundancy.

While taking into account your attendance record is also legitimate, the employer will be on thin ice if you suffer from a disability that leads to the absences. Equally the employer cannot take into account any absences because you took legitimate leave such as maternity, paternity or adoption leave.

Again the employer will need to have records that show your attendance levels are demonstrably worse than those of other employees, and should hold accurate information about the reasons for those absences. If you are in a position where your attendance record counts against you, it is legitimate to ask the employer to show that your attendance is worse than that of other employees. If that is the case, you could point out that you are being penalized for having been ill.

Could someone else be selected instead?

'Bumping'

If you feel that you have more to offer the organization than certain others whose jobs are not at risk, you could suggest that one of those others is made redundant instead of you and that you take over that person's job. Provided you have the necessary skills to do the job in question, there is no reason why this cannot happen.

This process is known as 'bumping' and occurs when the person in the job being made redundant takes over another role and it is the person in that other role who is made redundant. That person would still retain all redundancy rights. This is clearly not a practical proposition where your skills and experience are not easily transferable and it is your job that is not required. This is another reason why it is important to know who is in the redundancy pool.

What options other than redundancy have been considered?

Redundancy is usually a last resort for most employers and you should ask what other options have been considered. In larger organizations with divisional structures and employees operating in different business sectors, it is perfectly possible for employees in one part of the organization to be suffering a severe downturn in business while others are working inordinate amounts of overtime. The question that naturally arises is whether the required cost savings could be made by reducing overtime, but clearly in a sector where the demand is high this is unlikely to be a practical proposition. Of course where everyone is working in the same environment it should be the first action taken.

If agency or temporary staff are used by the company it would be reasonable to suggest that their services are dispensed with before laying off permanent employees. This would be one of the first considerations for most employers.

Another option for the employer might be to reorganize work in some way. If there is a need to reduce costs, however, reorganization still leaves the need for a saving in some respect. This could mean for example that the number of jobs remains the same but the size of those jobs and the associated pay levels are reduced. The employer would then have to offer the new jobs to the existing employees.

There is no prescribed way of doing this. The employer could just decide which jobs to offer to which people, but especially where large numbers of jobs are involved, what is often seen as the fairest approach is to ask employees to apply for those jobs. You may sometimes have heard people complaining that they are required to apply for their own jobs, and this is generally the reason. Some jobs may be ring-fenced – that is, not subject to the application process – or there might be rules restricting the number of jobs that have to be competed for, for instance by stating that anyone carrying out more than, say, 50 per cent of the new role will be slotted into that job rather than having to apply for it.

Assessment centres

The selection of candidates can be by competitive interview, through an assessment centre or by a combination of the two. An assessment centre usually involves a range of different types of tests, group activities and interviews. These can be run internally but are often provided by external companies. There is probably not a great deal you can do by way of preparation since the aim is to try and identify the knowledge, skills, competencies and experience required by the organization and you will either have what they are looking for or you will not.

Of course when these are used to identify potential cand-idates for redundancy you do have the advantage of generally knowing what the organization is looking for, so you can try to demonstrate that you have the required attributes. On the other hand, the organization's managers will also have a very good idea of your capabilities, so there is little scope for embellishing these.

Working reduced hours

The employer may consider asking you and others to work reduced hours with a commensurate reduction in pay. As this is a change to the contract of employment it needs to be agreed with everyone affected. If the employer just imposes such a change without agreement, this is likely to be a breach of the contract of employment and you may be able to take a claim to an employment tribunal.

What other jobs could I be considered for?

You have absolutely nothing to lose by suggesting other jobs you could be considered for. These need not be in the same type of work or location, provided you are prepared to retrain or relocate. Where the organization is a large one you may be able to suggest working in other parts of it, but this will clearly not apply in small companies. The employer must be prepared to consider suitable alternative employment and any related retraining.

What redundancy pay and severance payments will I be given?

If you are made redundant and have been employed for at least two years you have an entitlement to redundancy pay, subject to a statutory maximum amount that is reviewed annually. The details of this payment and how it is calculated are explained in more detail in Chapter 2. However, the employer can pay more than the statutory limit, and many do so. You need to be given clear information about the amounts that may be payable to you and how they have been calculated. This is likely to be a key consideration when deciding whether you would prefer to take redundancy or keep your job.

The golden rule

When you reach this stage of talking about the amount of money you are likely to be given, the golden rule is not to accept the first offer made. You should instead make a counter offer, bearing in mind that you will need to show a willingness to negotiate on this and so should ask for more than you would be prepared to settle for.

Realistically, where a number of people are being made redundant the employer might not have much scope for negotiation, but bear in mind that each settlement is on an individual basis so there is no reason why you should not try to get a better deal than that offered to your colleagues.

What to negotiate

Getting a better deal

Although there are legal minimum entitlements to notice (or pay in lieu of notice) and to redundancy pay, there may be plenty of scope for you to reach a better deal with your employer. The extent to which you can do this is likely to vary according to your seniority in the organization and also with the numbers being made redundant. Where there are mass redundancies your negotiating position is likely to be weakened. You may even be able to bring in an external solicitor to help in the negotiations, which may certainly be worth doing where large sums are involved.

The key tactic here, as mentioned above but worth repeating, is not to agree to the first deal you are offered. Ask to see any offer in writing, say that you will think it over and then come back with some of your own suggestions. Try to keep the relationship friendly and businesslike.

The top priority in any negotiation will usually be to try and get more money. You could simply try asking but it makes sense to try to come up with legitimate reasons why you should be paid more. If, for example, you were part of a sales force and the redundancy criteria related to sales volumes but there was a legitimate reason why you had not performed as well as others, perhaps because of an absence through sickness or training or because you had been allocated a sales area with less potential, then you might be able to argue that your bonus earnings were adversely affected and/or that the selection criteria were unfair. Criticizing the selection criteria also hints at possible legal action.

Another argument for more money could be length of service. If you have worked for the same organization for many years, you may be able to argue that it is unfair to give you just the statutory minimum. You could point out the possible effect on the organization's reputation.

One of the key factors to bear in mind in negotiating a redundancy settlement is that the money you are paid will have to support you until you find a new job. The more senior or specialist the role, the longer it is likely to take you to find a new job. If you think this process is likely to take six months, then you should be aiming for a package that will support you for that period.

Remember to check all the figures on any offer you get as simple clerical errors can result in under- or overpayment.

Bonuses

Where bonuses form part of your remuneration package and the employer excludes these from the redundancy package or offers a reduced payment, there is often scope for arguing that there were circumstances preventing you meeting your targets. Perhaps there has been a general decline in the market for your particular product or service. In large companies with several different divisions, it is not uncommon for one part of the company to be struggling for sales while another part remains very busy. There is inevitably a strong link between reduced sales and redundancies.

Benefits

You are entitled to retain any benefits during your notice period but you may also be able to negotiate to keep items such as laptops and mobile phones and retain other benefits such as medical insurance beyond this period. It is often possible to buy any company car at a very competitive price, such as its book value. The book value of the car is its value depreciated by a uniform amount each year. This rate of depreciation often does not reflect the market value of the car, which is usually more.

Ensure that you take into account all aspects of your employment package, including holidays, paid sick leave, share options, bonuses, sabbatical leave, medical insurance, company car, pension and so on. If you are over 50, you may be able to negotiate more money to boost your pension fund.

If you have a long notice period, for example more than three months, the employers might argue that you have a duty to seek to minimize your losses by seeking and accepting suitable alternative work. For this reason, if your employer discovers during negotiations that you have already lined up another well-paid job, the compensation that you are offered could be reduced drastically.

Precedents

You need to try and get information about what might have happened in relation to other redundancies. If, for example, more generous payments were made to other staff or in previous rounds of redundancy, these can be cited as a precedent.

Market practice

You may be able to get information about the practice in other organizations or in the sector generally, where this helps your case. There are publications, such as IDS (Incomes Data Services) reports, that occasionally publish surveys on such issues as redundancy practice within certain organizations.

Financial assistance for retraining

You may also be able to negotiate financial assistance for retraining as part of the redundancy package. Many larger employers will pay for outplacement and career counselling, typically up to around £3,000, as part of the package, and may also be willing to pay for any retraining recommended by those counsellors.

Tax

If you are fortunate enough to be given a redundancy payment in excess of the tax-free sum of £30,000, consider asking the organization to pay this amount into your pension so that you can keep your tax bill to the minimum.

Turning the screw

Although you should try to be as reasonable and professional as possible during the negotiation process, there may come a time when you have to start being a bit of a nuisance, especially if you consider that the terms you are being offered are not good enough. If there are a number of you in this position, the organization might be tempted to top-up the amounts being offered to avoid the danger of having to deal with lots of appeals and arguments. Even if you can benefit from the collective strength of a number of redundant employees, you should still remember that you have to fight your own corner and bear in mind that the employer might be prepared to make a concession if it only affects one person rather than several.

Finally, one reason for trying to keep relationships amicable is that you would probably want to leave the organization with a good reference.

Compromise agreements

One way to try and negotiate a better deal is to offer to sign what is known as a compromise agreement. This is an agreement between you and the organization that you will not bring a claim against the organization. By signing such an agreement you are in effect signing away any right to bring a claim for unfair dismissal, wrongful dismissal (which is not the same as unfair dismissal but is dismissal in breach of the employment contract), discrimination, breach of contract, loss of earnings or other causes.

If, therefore, you feel you have any strong claim against the organization you will need to think carefully about whether you should sign such an agreement. The only reason you would do so is in return for additional compensation, so this would need to be at a level that would make it not worth your while to pursue any claim.

In considering how much you might be prepared to settle for you need to have some idea of the likely compensation if you were to win a case at an employment tribunal. The calculation of compensation is considered in Chapter 5.

For a compromise agreement to be legal you must have received independent legal advice on it and the employer is expected to pay for this, a sum of up to £500 being typical. However, it is possible that the advice might cost more than this, in which case you might be liable for any additional costs. The agreement must also relate specifically to the issue in dispute: that is, the redundancy.

It is quite likely that, in these circumstances, the employer would recommend that you go to the organization's solicitors. However, as there is the danger that they may not be completely independent, you may wish to find your own solicitor.

In addition to specifying the amount to be paid to you, it is common practice for the organization to include a number of additional conditions in any compromise agreement. These can include, for example, that you will not make any derogatory remarks about the organization or its staff after leaving, that you will not compete with the organization, that you will not disclose confidential information, and that you will return all property, files and any other data held to the organization immediately. You may also be required to resign from any directorships held.

You could also insist that the employer insert a clause within the agreement guaranteeing you a good reference, or even that a reference is attached to the agreement.

Key points

1. Understand the power of your negotiating position.

2. Prepare thoroughly by reading all relevant policies, procedures and letters.

3. Keep discussions and meetings as amicable and professional as possible, at least in the early stages.

4. Do not hesitate to ask questions to get as much information as possible about the redundancy process.

5. Never accept the first offer.

6. Check all figures given to you.

7. Consider signing a compromise agreement provided you can negotiate a better redundancy deal.

5

Getting compensation for unfair dismissal

The meaning of unfair dismissal

When you are made redundant this is a dismissal. For this type of dismissal to be fair the employer must have satisfied the following conditions:

- It must be for the reason stated, ie redundancy, and this should not be used as an excuse for a different reason, such as capability to do the job.

- You must have been consulted prior to the redundancy and this must have been genuine consultation.

- You should have been given adequate time to consider the situation, and although this is not defined, anything less than one week would probably not satisfy this requirement.

- If over 20 people are being made redundant over a period of 90 days, the employer should have formally consulted any trade unions or employee representatives.

- Your selection for redundancy should be based on fair and objective criteria and not on any discriminatory criteria such as sex, race, age, disability or trade union membership.

- If there is suitable alternative employment available, you should have been offered this and been given the opportunity to try out this alternative work (provided you have two years' service).

- You should have been given an opportunity to appeal.

- You must have been given your contractual or statutory notice period or pay in lieu of the notice.

- You should have received redundancy pay provided you have two years' continuous employment with this employer.

- You should not have been pregnant or on maternity leave at the time of the redundancy.

It is likely, though by no means certain, that if the employer has failed to meet any of the above conditions, any redundancy dismissal will be unfair, although whether or not it is will be for an employment tribunal to determine, if the issue gets that far.

It may also be the case that the dismissal could be unfair if the employer does not allow you to be accompanied by a colleague or trade union representative, although this is not certain as the law does not specifically provide for this. However, if the organization's procedure allows you to be accompanied, or if others have been accompanied and you have not, then not allowing you a companion is likely to be unfair. See Chapter 2 for more information.

Business transfers

If your organization has been taken over by another and you have been made redundant as a result, then this is likely to be an automatically unfair dismissal. However, the employer has a powerful defence against such a claim as he or she can argue that any redundancy might be for economic, technical or organizational reasons, and dismissal for these reasons are all legitimate. Be aware also that if you refuse to transfer to the new employer this is likely to be regarded as a resignation by you and would not be regarded as redundancy.

Claiming unfair dismissal

You cannot take an unfair dismissal claim to an employment tribunal unless you have at least one year's service with your employer. However this time limit does not apply where any form of discrimination is involved so if, for example, you feel that you have been unfairly selected because you are of a certain age or race, have a disability or similar reasons, then you can bring a claim regardless of how long you have been with the organization.

Discrimination claims are the employer's greatest fear because not only does the service condition not apply but the compensation awarded is unlimited and can be huge. With normal unfair dismissal claims there is a statutory limit, currently £66,200, but with discrimination claims compensation can run into hundreds of thousands (see the example in Chapter 4) although it has to be stressed that these cases are the exceptions. They are the ones that make the newspaper headlines.

There are certain other circumstances where the service condition does not apply, such as being dismissed after blowing the whistle on the employer or because you tried to assert one of your statutory rights, but these will not generally apply to redundancy dismissal, unless redundancy is not the real reason for the dismissal.

You should also note that the one year's service includes your notice period, so that, for example, if you are sacked after nine months but your contract entitles you to three months' notice, adding these together might give you the required length of service to bring a claim.

Employment tribunals

If you feel that you have been unfairly dismissed you should first raise the issue with your employer, who will generally be aware of the implications of having to deal with an unfair dismissal. If you cannot get a satisfactory resolution of the issue than you might have to consider going to an employment tribunal.

Employment tribunals are judicial bodies that try to settle disputes between employers and employees. They were originally established to provide quick solutions to workplace disputes without the complicated legal trappings of the courts but unfortunately such is the complexity of modern employment law that they have been hijacked by the lawyers.

Claims for unfair dismissal must usually be submitted to the Employment Tribunal Service within three months of the date of dismissal, although in certain circumstances this timescale can be extended. Late claims are generally ruled out of time.

These tribunals can also consider claims for breach of contract up to a value of £25,000, for example where the employer may be resisting paying a bonus to which you think you are contractually entitled. If the amounts involved are higher than this, then you would have to take the matter to a county court.

The advantage for you of going to an employment tribunal is that it will not generally cost you anything, whereas it could potentially cost the employer a great deal, not just in compensation if the case is lost but also in the time and legal costs involved in preparing the case and then attending the tribunal. There is also the bad publicity. For this reason most cases are settled outside the tribunal.

Whether or not you actually intend to go ahead with a tribunal case, the mere threat of doing so gives you added leverage. You also need to bear in mind that going to a tribunal can be a stressful experience for you, especially if you intend to defend yourself, and also for the employer. You could of course engage a solicitor on a 'no-win, no-fee' basis.

Making a claim

Full information on how to take a claim to a tribunal can be found on the Employment Tribunals' website www. employmenttribunals.gov.uk. As a first step you will have to complete a form ET1, which can look quite daunting as it is a long form. However, it is relatively straightforward to complete. There is one section where you have to explain what your claim is about and it is usually better to attach pages prepared on a computer or word processor rather than try to fill in the boxes on the form. Once completed this form will need to be sent to the regional employment tribunal office relating to your place of work.

In the next stage of the process the form is sent to your employer, who is described as the respondent and who must reply to the claim within 28 days. This response will then be sent to you or your representative. At this stage you can then ask the employer for any more information, such as copies of any letters or e-mails or any relevant policies, and for clarification of any points. If the employer does not provide this information within a reasonable time frame the employment tribunal can require him or her to do so.

All claims are automatically sent to the Advisory Conciliation and Arbitration Service (ACAS) and someone from them will get in touch with you to see if there is any possibility of the claim being settled before it is referred to the tribunal. Experience suggests that they will generally try to suggest a settlement that is midway between what the employer is offering and what you are seeking. In trying to decide whether or not to agree to a settlement you need to try to assess the likely level of compensation you might get if successful.

Levels of award

There are three different elements used in assessing the level of compensation to be paid for unfair dismissal:

- A basic award, calculated by taking into account your age and years of service on the same basis as a redundancy payment, so that, for example, if you are 35 years old with five years' service then the basic award will be up to five times the weekly statutory maximum figure, which is currently £380 per week. This can be reduced for certain reasons, such as you unreasonably rejecting suitable alternative employment or being partly responsible for your own dismissal.

- A compensatory award is intended to compensate you for any financial loss arising from the dismissal, including any loss of pay and benefits from the date of your dismissal until the tribunal hearing, plus compensation for the time it is likely to take you to get another job, taking into account the kind of work you do and the demand for that type of work. A maximum of £66,200 can be paid under this heading but this amount can be reduced for certain reasons, such as unreasonable behaviour by you, including not making any effort to find a new job. If you have already found another job you would be unlikely to receive any payment under this heading.

- An additional award, which is payable if the employer is asked to take you back but refuses to do so. Compensation in these circumstances can be between 26 and 52 weeks' pay, capped at the statutory maximum rate.

Awards where discrimination is involved

As stated elsewhere in this book, where discrimination is involved the tribunal can also make an additional award for injury to feelings and, although there is no limit to the amount that can be paid in such cases, realistically the figure is unlikely to be much more than £5,000–£10,000, unless there has been a history of sustained abuse of a long-serving employee. This, of course, is still a significant sum.

As with negotiating a redundancy package, if you are offered an amount to settle, do not accept the first offer, even if you receive a solicitor's letter stating that the offer is a final one and has to be accepted by a given deadline. You should ignore this and instead put in your own counter-offer at a level higher than you would be prepared to accept, and then negotiate on this figure.

These kinds of discussions can take place right up to the day of the employment tribunal, and settlements are often reached at the tribunal offices before going into the hearing.

Going to a tribunal

Before a tribunal hearing there will be a need for the parties to agree the relevant paperwork to be put before the tribunal. This is known as a 'bundle' and is a paginated collection of all papers and witness statements.

Most tribunal panels comprise three members, including a legally qualified chairperson and two others, one from a trade union background and one from an employers' organization background. The proceedings are formal, with both sides giving evidence and being subject to cross-examination. When this is concluded both parties will be given an opportunity to make a closing address and the panel will then retire to make a judgement.

If you represent yourself you are likely to find that the tribunal is quite supportive and will ask questions on your behalf.

Wrongful dismissal

It was stated above that to bring a case of unfair dismissal before a tribunal you need to have at least one year's service with your employer. However, you do not need this to bring a claim of wrongful dismissal. Wrongful dismissal arises if you have been dismissed in breach of the contract of employment. This could arise, for example, if the employer failed to follow the stages in a disciplinary procedure that was part of your contract, or failed to apply an agreed redundancy and severance scheme.

Damages can be paid to compensate you for any loss of earnings, including contractual benefits, but you would be expected to 'mitigate your loss' by finding a new job and this would be taken into account in assessing the amount payable.

Realistically these types of claims are comparatively rare because you would have to prove that the employer was in breach of the contract of employment and this would have to be done through the courts, not via an employment tribunal. Given the likely costs and the uncertainty of outcome it is unlikely to be a wise path to take unless the sums involved are substantial.

Constructive dismissal

In some circumstances the employer might feel that one way of reducing the workforce without having to make redundancy payments would be to treat employees so badly that they feel they have no option but to resign. These examples are rare but they do happen. This is known as constructive dismissal and arises when employees resign but feel that they have no option but to do so because of an employer's unreasonable behaviour. However, to bring such a claim you would first have to resign and then prove your case in a court of law, so it is not a recommended option. If your employers want you to go and you resign, you solve their problem for them.

Key points

1. Losing your job because of redundancy is a dismissal and has to meet a number of conditions to be fair.

2. In the case of a business transfer (ie a takeover or a merger) a redundancy because of the transfer is likely to be unfair.

3. You need to have been employed within that organization for at least one year before you can bring a claim of unfair dismissal to an employment tribunal.

4. Where discrimination is involved there is no requirement for you to have a year's service to bring a claim.

5. An employment tribunal claim has to be raised within three months of the event complained of.

6. The maximum compensation payable is currently £66,200 (reviewed annually) except for discrimination cases, where there is no limit.

7. Wrongful dismissal is different from unfair dismissal and is dismissal in breach of the contract of employment; no minimum period of service is required to bring such a claim.

8. Constructive dismissal arises where you resign but claim you had no option because of the employer's unreasonable behaviour.

6

Managing your money

What you should leave with

The basis for calculating redundancy payments was set out in Chapter 2. How much you actually leave with depends on your age and length of service, what you were previously earning, how much notice you were given and how generous your employer was.

If you have five years' service for example, and you are aged between 22 and 41, you would get a redundancy payment of five times £380, ie £1,900, assuming your employer paid the statutory maximum but no more, plus five weeks' notice pay if your contractual notice period does not exceed this. This will have to last until you get another job. The good news of course is that these payments will generally be tax free (but not if you work your notice period). You may, however, be able to supplement your income with state benefits.

You should be given your redundancy pay automatically on leaving, but if not you should ask for it in writing. If you do not get a reply then you will need to take the matter to an employment tribunal. You need to do this within three months of your employment ending.

On leaving you should also make sure that you are given your P45, written details of the redundancy package and a good reference.

What you should do with your money

The first consideration is the best way of managing the money you are given. Of course it really depends on how much you get. Many redundancy payments are likely to be relatively modest unless you have long service or get enhanced payments from the employer.

If you have got a long period of service behind you with a potential maximum of up to £1,400 (30 weeks times £380) plus up to 12 weeks' notice pay, the sum paid out could be a tidy sum. While it may be tempting to spend any significant amounts, you need to bear in mind that you may need all of this to meet your living costs until you get a new job. Depending on the kind of job you do and the industry sector you are in, this could take several months and you need to allow for this. It could of course be an opportunity to pay off any debts and, as these can be expensive to service, this should be a priority.

Career counsellors

The question is often asked about whether it would be worthwhile to pay for the services of a career counselling company. This really depends on how confident you are about your ability to conduct a job search, complete a CV or application form and cope with selection tests and interviews. Obviously you have taken the right step in reading this book!

If you decide that you need some detailed support and consider that one of these companies might be able to help, the first thing to do is to shop around, as the fees involved can be substantial. There are also other support options you should consider. Some professional bodies provide career counselling and support. For example, the Institute of Directors have advisers who can give pointers on such issues as conducting a job search and CV preparation, and an organization like this should be your first port of call before committing an outlay of thousands of pounds for no guaranteed return.

Another possibly worthwhile expense could be to retrain for a different job or career, or even to set up your own business or buy a franchise.

If you are of an age where you can consider early retirement or if you can afford to save or invest your redundancy lump sum, you should consult an independent financial adviser (IFA). Although any initial meeting will be free, any investments will be subject to the IFA's commission and fees. You can get advice from your bank or building society but their staff are usually restricted to promoting their own investments and so may offer a smaller range of options.

Other good sources of information about investments, and especially savings rates, are the newspapers and various financial websites such as 'Martin's Moneytips' (www. moneysavingexpert.com), the latter being worth looking at whether or not you are made redundant. Given recent developments in the banking sector, however, it is best not to put all your eggs in one basket.

Benefits you may be eligible for

There are a number of state benefits that you might be able to claim during any period of unemployment before finding a new job. Most benefits are managed by the Department for

Work and Pensions (DWP) through Jobcentre Plus offices, which are located in major towns or which can be contacted over the telephone or the internet. Other agencies are involved in certain other benefits, such as Her Majesty's Revenue and Customs (HMRC) who deal with working tax credits, guardian's allowance and child benefit.

The main benefits you may be able to claim are outlined below.

Jobseeker's Allowance (JSA)

You can claim this if you are not working or working less than 16 hours per week and provided that you are:

- capable of working;
- available for work;
- actively seeking work;
- below state pension age.

This means that you have to sign-on at Jobcentre Plus (a government agency) and attend regular meetings. You must sign a jobseeker's agreement to get JSA. This includes information about the times and days you will look for work, what sort of work you will look for, how you will go about it and what you will do to improve your chances of getting a job. The adviser can change any limitations you put on jobs if he or she thinks they are unreasonable.

There are two kinds of allowance: contribution-based Jobseeker's Allowance and income-based Jobseeker's Allowance.

Contribution-based Jobseeker's Allowance

You may get contribution-based Jobseeker's Allowance if you have paid or been credited with Class 1 National Insurance

(NI) contributions in the relevant tax years. You need to have worked for at least six months and be earning above the lower earnings limit for NI contributions (currently £95 per week). Self-employed contributions will not generally qualify you for contribution-based Jobseeker's Allowance.

This is a weekly rate based on your age as follows:

Age	Amount
16–24	£50.95
25 or over	£64.30

This allowance is not means-tested and the status of your partner is not taken into account, but your payments might be reduced if you are getting a pension or have part-time earnings, and you will not get anything at all until the notice period covered by your redundancy payment has expired.

Income-based Jobseeker's Allowance

This is based on your income and savings. You may get this if you have not paid enough NI contributions (or you have only paid contributions for self-employment) and you are on a low income.

The current maximum weekly rates are as follows:

Status	Amount
Single people aged 16–24	£50.95
Single people aged 25 or over	£64.30
Couples and civil partnerships (both aged 18 or over)	£100.95
Lone parents (aged under 18)	£50.95
Lone parents (aged 18 or over)	£64.30

Your payments might be reduced if you receive income from part-time employment. You will get less if you have savings over £6,000. If you have savings over £16,000 you probably will not qualify.

If your partner works 24 hours or more a week on average, you cannot usually get income-based JSA (contribution-based JSA isn't affected). If they work less than 24 hours, it may affect how much you get.

Other benefits

If you are on income-based JSA, you will be able to get housing benefit to help with rent and council tax benefit, which reduces your council tax bill. You will also be entitled to other help such as free prescriptions and children's free school meals. These might also apply to contribution-based JSA, but this depends on your income.

You will not get any help to pay your mortgage for the first 13 weeks after you have been made redundant, but after that JSA, employment and support allowance and income support can all help to pay the interest on your mortgage, but not the capital.

Mortgage payment support

If you are lucky enough or have had the foresight to get mortgage payment protection insurance you should be able to make a claim for this, redundancy being precisely the sort of situation such a policy should protect you against.

However, these policies have a reputation for being very difficult to claim on and you are likely to have to prove that you are actively looking for work. They also generally only pay out for a period of 12 months, but this should be long enough for you to find another job.

If you are having problems paying your mortgage, the first step should be to contact your lender to see if you can reduce your payments, have a payment holiday, extend the term, or maybe just pay the interest for a period if you have a repayment mortgage that includes both interest and capital repayments.

Mortgage providers have stated that they are prepared to be more flexible in agreeing to these kinds of arrangement. If this does not work there are government initiatives designed to help people in this position and to try and reduce the number of repossessions. This includes a mortgage rescue scheme administered by your local housing authority and aimed at those in 'priority need'. This could include people who have dependent children, single pregnant women, the elderly or people with disabilities. This is also means tested and there are a number of other criteria that you would have to meet. There is also a homeowner's mortgage support scheme aimed at those who have had a temporary drop in income but who are likely to be able to get their finances back on track in the future. This scheme allows mortgage repayments to be reduced for a period of up to two years, but is only operated by certain lenders. It would not apply to you if your lender does not participate in the scheme.

Other benefits such as income support could be available to certain people such as those who are sick or disabled, but only a minority of people will qualify for these.

Non-financial support

There is support other than financial support that is also available from both commercial and government services to people looking for work. If you are losing your job as part of mass redundancies or a major plant closure, it is likely that you will be offered advice by Jobcentre Plus or the Regional Development Agency. They may help you look for work, provide access to training, and give advice on managing your finances or on starting a business. Jobcentre Plus will take your details and arrange an appointment with an adviser to talk about why you are unemployed and what sort of job you are looking for.

Pensions

If you are at the right age you might consider that redundancy offers an opportunity to retire early. On retirement you will receive both the pension and a lump sum payment, and will usually have to make a decision about how much of the pension should be taken as the lump sum, as this will have an impact on the size of the regular pension payments. If you decide to do this you obviously need to check your pension position, assuming you have one. Pensions and the decisions relating to them are complex and this is an area where you will almost certainly need to get advice.

Pension schemes are of two broad types: defined-contribution schemes and defined-benefit schemes.

Defined-contribution schemes

A defined-contribution scheme is one that pays a pension where the contributions made by the employer and the employee are standard and the amounts paid by the pension scheme depend on the performance of the investments bought by these contributions. All you can be certain of in such a scheme is the level of the contributions made.

Over the years your contributions will build into your pension pot, which can easily be transferred into another scheme when you leave the organization or may be left with the pension company used by your former employer. If, on redundancy, you are due to receive a payment under an occupational pension scheme within 90 weeks of your dismissal, your redundancy payment could be reduced. This is an area where independent financial advice is probably essential.

Defined-benefit schemes

In defined-benefit schemes the pension will depend on how long you have worked for your employer, your earnings and the rules of the scheme. The important aspect of this type of scheme is that the level of benefit is guaranteed by the employer and you know what you will get regardless of how well the investments in the scheme have performed. Final salary schemes are of this type.

More and more schemes of this type in the private sector are closing because of the requirement on the employer to ensure that there is enough money in the pension fund to meet the pension commitments. If the company goes broke there might not be enough money left in the pension scheme for the organization to be able to pay the pensions in full. These schemes have generally continued in the public sector.

Depending on the rules of the scheme you may be able to retire early with a reduced pension. Some schemes, especially in the public sector, give added years where you retire early because of redundancy. Any payments would be in addition to redundancy payments.

If you are not old enough to retire you may be able to:

▪ transfer your pension to another scheme, although this may be difficult to do outside the public sector with a defined benefit scheme, or transfer it to your own personal pension scheme;

▪ leave the pension with your former employer and receive it when you retire, known as a deferred pension;

■ be given a transfer value, which is a lump sum to be invested in a different personal pension scheme;

■ be offered a refund of contributions if you have only been a member of the scheme for a relatively short time.

Taxation

The key points to note in relation to taxation are:

■ Usually the first £30,000 of redundancy pay is tax free.

■ There may be a tax and National Insurance liability where you are given pay in lieu of notice as this is regarded as normal pay rather than a redundancy payment, but whether or not tax is payable in this situation depends on the wording of your employment contract.

■ If you have to pay tax it counts against your tax bill in the year you receive the money, not when you were made redundant.

■ You may be able to reduce your tax liability by paying some of your redundancy pay into your pension.

■ Jobseeker's allowance is treated as taxable income and while tax is not payable immediately it will be counted against your earnings for the tax year.

Further information

For advice on savings, pensions and money management

www.moneysavingexpert.com
www.moneymagpie.com
www.worksmart.com

For information and advice on redundancy and redundancy pay

www.direct.gov.uk
The Advisory, Conciliation and Arbitration Service (ACAS)
www.acas.org.uk
www.berr.gov.uk
www.worksmart.com
Citizens' Advice Bureaux www.adviceguide.org.uk

For information on benefits

www.direct.gov.uk
www.jobcentreplus.gov.uk
Citizens' Advice Bureaux www.adviceguide.org.uk
Jobseeker's Allowance: telephone 0800 055 6688 (8am – 6pm Monday to Friday); a textphone service is available if you have a speech or hearing impairment (0800 023 4888)

For training and retraining and advice with conducting a job search

Local Jobcentre Plus offices
www.redundancyhelp.co.uk
www.direct.gov.uk/careersadvice
Various professional organizations (for members eg Institute of Directors)

The TUC's Know Your Rights line

This offers a wide range of employment advice and free leaflets about rights and redundancy, among other topics.

Key points

1. Redundancy pay (see Appendix 1 for a guide to entitlements) should be paid automatically when you end your job, but will have to last until you find another position.

2. Career counsellors can provide advice, but shop around as they can be expensive; it is often better to contact professional bodies that provide counselling and support.

3. Available benefits include the Jobseeker's Allowance.

4. In the private sector, defined-contribution pension schemes are now more common than defined-benefit schemes.

5. The first £30,000 of redundancy pay (but not of pay in lieu of notice) is usually tax free; if tax is levied, it counts against the year in which you receive the money, which may not be the year in which you were made redundant.

7

Living in the present

In this chapter we come fully up to date. It is time to start to assess your career options, and to do this you need to think through what skills you have and what kind of life you want to aim for, in order to see what options might be available to you. Once you have identified them, you can research what is possible and think about training opportunities too. You can then set targets for yourself and start moving on with a plan of action for the future.

Assessing your career options

Success and fulfilment at work don't always fall into place by chance. This is a time for you to pause, take a step back and begin to think through the options available. One of the side effects of finding yourself out of work is that you can use the time to plan what will come next. This is one of the advantages of being made redundant.

This may be a whole new experience for you. It may well be that you have not ever assessed your career choices so overtly or rationally before. Many people drift through different jobs without a clear plan. If this is the case, you need to be aware that this kind of thinking and researching takes time and effort to be done properly. Be warned though that it may prompt you to question key aspects of the way you have been living your life. It can be a very rewarding project to carry out successfully and can bring about big changes.

There are several parts to this process. First you need to consider what you have in your portfolio. By 'portfolio' we mean all the skills, knowledge and achievements gained from your employment, education and training endeavours to date. This is where you are at the present time. The next step is to look forward to what you would like to have, work at, know or be in the future – this will point to your future goals. The third stage is when you can work out how to get there, by considering all the different routes available. This makes it sound as though the process of planning your career is tidy, neat and definite. In reality it will probably be messy, unclear and subject to a lot of change and revision.

You may not be able to go back into an exactly similar job to the one you have just left. It may be necessary to take a step backwards in order to move forward. If your priority is to get a job, any job, then you may need to set your sights a little lower to start with. This is particularly true when there is a lot of competition for jobs, for instance if a lot of people were made redundant from one type of role in one locality.

The points from Chapter 3 about reclaiming a positive frame of mind begin to be particularly important from now on. In order to think about your future, never mind find a new job, you need to be feeling positive and upbeat. Garnish all your self-confidence, polish up your hopes for the future and let's get to work.

Identifying your skills

What are you offering to an employer? Recently you have been more concerned with what you have lost or are giving up, but now you must turn your mind in the other direction. What special things can you contribute to a company or organization that make you worth employing? Just being able to do the job is not enough. Wanting the job only puts you on a level with every other applicant. This point cannot be emphasized enough – you need to be able to sell yourself on the basis of what you are offering.

The following list contains descriptive words for skills and abilities that are in demand in the job market. Use it to help you identify your own particular assets by marking the ones that you feel apply to you. First read through and put a tick by the ones that you think describe you (the first column). Perhaps they have been highlighted in relation to you by employers or supervisors in the past. No one is good at everything on that list but it should prompt you to think about your own abilities. Add more that occur to you as you go through the list.

	I am	I enjoy being	I would like to be
Able to work alone			
Accurate			
Adaptable			
Alert			
Approachable			
Articulate			
Calm			
Capable			
Cautious			
Collaborative			
Committed			

	I am	I enjoy being	I would like to be
Communicative			
Competent			
Cooperative			
Creative			
Decisive			
Dedicated			
Determined			
Dynamic			
Enthusiastic			
Flexible			
Friendly			
Good at deadlines			
Good managerially			
Handy			
Hardworking			
Humorous			
Innovative			
Lively			
Loyal			
Methodical			
Motivating			
Optimistic			
Organized			
Patient			
Perceptive			
Polite			
Practical			
Proactive			
Punctual			
Quick to learn			
Reliable			
Responsible			
Self-motivated			
Sensible			
Sensitive			
Serious-minded			

	I am	I enjoy being	I would like to be
Sociable			
Steadfast			
Strong			
Tactful			
Thorough			
Versatile			
(Add more words here)			

Now review your list. Do the words you have ticked all describe similar strengths or do they show you to be a very varied character? Does any particular type of work spring to mind as you read your list of adjectives? Do you see a pattern emerging of the kind of work that you are ideally suited to or is the picture more mixed?

Now go through the list again but this time put a tick in the second column of your list to show which are the things you most enjoy. You may be good at statistical analysis but still be sick to death of working with figures. You may be in a job with little opportunity for creativity but still enjoy it the most when it does occur. If you can make notes of what you really enjoy or want to do more of, this can help to guide you in the choices you make for the future.

Are you happy with the way you are depicted with these words or is some area of your skills left out? Do you wish you could add different words? Go through the list again and now mark those words that you would like to describe you. Are they very different to the ones you have marked in the first two columns? Perhaps there is a link here to some kind of new skill development through training that you could plan for?

Take action!

Really focus on this activity, as knowing your strengths and skills will be crucial when applying for your next job.

Lifestyle choices

There are various options that could be possible for you in the future. These are the main variations:

- working for an employer, part time or full time, permanent or temporary employment;

- self-employment, literally employing yourself, making or selling products or services;

- freelance or consultancy work, where you are paid by clients for fixed periods or pieces of work;

- studying full or part time or on a training course;

- doing no paid activity – travelling, studying for pleasure or taking time off;

- pursuing an interest or hobby;

- voluntary activity;

- retirement;

- any combination of the above.

For some people, redundancy offers the chance just to take some time off. Volunteering can be an option if you are not desperate for money. If you have not had much work experience, have been laid off for some time or you are trying to find work in a new field, you may want to consider doing some voluntary work to help you gain more relevant, recent experience.

Voluntary work can be full or part time. It could be a fixed-term option perhaps for six months or a year, making an unpaid work contribution to a charity, or a permanent option if you can afford it, perhaps living off any redundancy payment whilst you do so. Pick a cause that you respect and believe in so that your values dovetail with theirs.

This can be a way to gain experience in a different field, do some good work and learn a lot about yourself whilst doing so. It provides a purpose, company with a new team of colleagues, a glimpse of a different sector of the economy and the chance of a good reference at the end of it. It may open up a whole new career or at least give you a wider perspective on paid work generally.

Adding to your interests in life to enhance your portfolio, rather than work at it – for instance, studying art part-time for pleasure – is something that could turn into an income-generator in the future. Gemma took a jewellery course when she was laid off from a call centre. She lived off her redundancy payout for a year. At the end of that time, she joined forces with a new friend from the course and started a craft business, selling their jewellery through a local clothes shop.

There is a trade-off here between time and money. There are lots of ways to spend your time, but you also need to calculate what you need to earn in order to maintain the minimum lifestyle that you would be prepared or able to live with.

Do you have some ideas about how you would like your life to be in the future? It may be that one of the options is a clear front-runner for your first choice at the moment.

Exercise

Get a blank piece of paper and a few coloured pencils. Use a spider diagram or spider-gram to take a look at your thoughts. Turn the paper sideways (landscape) and write in the middle some word or phrase about your career. Now put down your main thoughts in the form of branches radiating out from this central point. Use a different coloured pencil for each branch that you draw.

As you look at these main thoughts (or 'legs' of the spider) let other more detailed points occur to you. Add them off each leg as sub-branches and see where your thoughts take you. This tool is a useful way of enhancing your creative powers. It allows your brain to range freely around a topic, being stimulated by the colours you have used, generating yet more ideas by what it sees. A great little book on this topic is *How to Mind Map* by Tony Buzan (Thorsons, 2002).

Write down on this diagram what motivates you in your life. Have a branch for money, one for home life, one for status, one for relationships, one for social contacts and whatever other aspects represent things you want. Everyone's diagram will look quite different as we all value things differently. Make connections between aspects that affect each other, for instance you might connect up 'family' with the money branch as you need income to support family members in different ways.

This can be added to as you reflect on what you have put down. Revisit this page often to add to and amend what you have written, as these plans can evolve over time. These spider diagrams work by encouraging your brain to get creative so you might be surprised by what emerges from your thoughts. When you look at your picture, what pops out at you as being your main priorities? What sort of balance have you struck between work and non-work?

Take action!

Spider diagrams can help you come up with ideas on any subject. Make use of them.

Career options

Sometimes talking through your ideas is the easiest way to properly 'see' your options. What you want to do is reconcile what you have to offer with what you want, and then balance this with how much you need to survive. You could talk with a family member, a friend or an ex-colleague, or get a careers adviser to help you. There is a national careers advice line, which you may find helps to point you in the right direction. Their website is www.careersadvice.direct.gov.uk, or you can call them on 0800 100 900 and speak to an adviser. Many careers advisers charge for an in-depth consultation but you may find some free advice available in your area too.

Researching your choices

When you have some idea of the different options that might be possibilities, you can start to do some research. If you are sure that working full time is the option that you want, you can start to think about what sort of jobs you will apply for and where to find them. Don't just dash around madly though. Take a little time to plan what you intend to do.

Start by making a plan of what you want to find out. For example:

■ possible training in IT skills;

■ new job in clerical work;

■ complete change of career.

This way you push yourself to think specifically about how you are going to find out more, and this will prompt you in to action.

Retraining

It may be the right time to think about retraining or going back to college. For many people a period after redundancy presents an opportunity to return to learning. The substantial investment of time and energy needed might be possible when you find yourself with nothing in particular lined up as the next step. It may be one of the few times in your life when you are not automatically moving from job to job seamlessly.

■ Is there some work that interests you that requires studying at a higher level?

■ Did you miss out on doing a degree and always regret it?

■ Have you seen colleagues promoted over you because of their qualifications?

■ Do you want to test out how bright you are?

■ Is there a subject that you have always longed to be able to study?

There could be new skills that you would like to learn, or a trade such as electrical work or bricklaying. Studying options are much more varied now than they were in the past. Many colleges also offer a distance-learning option where you can study part or all of the course from home, using materials available on the internet or sent to you by mail. Some people prefer to learn on their own by themselves in a self-learning programme. Examples could be using specific study materials such as books and CDs from a library to learn a new language, or using manuals with your computer at home to learn more about IT applications.

There are pros and cons of training as an option:

Advantages	Disadvantages
Learn new skills	Time-consuming to do a full course
Meet new people	Needs commitment, ability and hard work
Stimulate your brain	You have to be accepted on to the course
Can enhance your career	You may not enjoy it
Gives a sense of achievement	You could fail the course
Could be affordable	Expensive, requires fees and subsistence has to be paid for

Setting your targets

You may have some ideas now of what you want to find out more about and how to do this. Setting yourself targets in the form of an action plan will keep you up to the mark and motivated.

Use the table below to set yourself some headings, tasks, desired outcomes and deadlines. It can be fine to plan some work but without a time when it has to be done, you may find yourself drifting without getting any progress made.

The kind of headings that you might want to include are:

- Work – to take your job search forward.

- Training and education – courses or retraining that you might be considering.

- Other plans – such as travel or pursuing some interest.

- Volunteering – possibilities of working without pay.

- Networking/contacts – to make links and provide information.

- Social – to keep you going and not isolated.

- Health – to maintain fitness.

- Support – other activities that may be helpful eg meeting up with colleagues who have also been made redundant.

Put a few different tasks under each heading, break them down into the specific results you are hoping for and then put the deadline in place. Make sure that you set yourself a reasonable time span for doing each task. In this way you are turning your future plan into a project to work on. This will help you focus and prioritize.

An example could be:

Heading	Task	What I will achieve	Deadline
Education	Explore degree courses	Read prospectuses for all universities in my area	End of November

Task	What I will achieve	By when

You can start to follow up each of these action points according to the deadline you have set for yourself. Each part of your research will tell you more about which of your options will bring you the better outcome so that you can make choices between them.

Questions and answers

Q. I am desperate to study history, which is a lifelong dream, and it seems I have the time to do it now but I am not eligible for any grant and the costs seem too high.

A. Have you considered studying with the Open University or some other distance-learning college? Although courses will take longer studied this way, they are set up for adult learners, allow you to work full or part time while you study, and give you a great flexibility if you need to take a break from the course in the middle for any reason. All the Open University courses are modular so you can easily stop the course and restart it again if you need to. You may well also find that if you are on a low income that you could be eligible for one of its grants to help with the finances too. See www.open.ac.uk to find out more.

Q. I went straight into work from school and have never done a plan of any sort for my career. I didn't even know I had a career! Since my redundancy, I think I would like to retrain as a nurse but I feel very unconfident about finding out more in case I am not suitable.

A. Don't let a lack of confidence hold you back. This could be the one opportunity in your life to follow your dreams. A great source of objective, current information about jobs and the qualifications needed for them at any age is www.connexions-direct.com/Jobs4u.

Read all about the area that interests you then contact the training councils or professional organizations listed there to find out about the different ways in to the jobs available. They all have websites that will tell you more, eg The Royal College of Nursing at www.rcn.org.uk.

Q. I find all this planning quite difficult. It seems that there are so many options and possibilities open to me. I have ideas about being self-employed but it would be risky financially. How do I know the right thing to do next?

A. Life would be much simpler if there was a right answer to career dilemmas. But there isn't. All you can do is get your list of possibilities and try to evaluate them. It sounds as though some sort of compromise would work best for you. Could you work part-time whilst trying out your self-employed ideas? Rather than take a big risk, take a smaller one and cover your essential expenditure with a regular but smaller income whilst trying to make it on your own for the rest of the week. Even if it all goes wrong, you can always change track again. Some of the most successful entrepreneurs had several false starts before they struck gold.

Key points

1. View managing your career as an exciting new project.

2. Dare to dream. Think big and think differently now you have the chance to make changes.

3. Try to identify patterns or themes from your past career.

4. Monitor job sites on the internet to see what kind of work is available.

5. Keep your options open; it is rare to find one perfect path.

8

Starting again

In this chapter you will be led into starting your next step. You have come up with some targets, now you can begin work on making them a reality. Your state of mind and outlook are crucial. It is also time to look at the way your life is organized so that all aspects support your endeavours.

Preparing a CV is the first activity that needs attention, and how that CV is presented is a key factor. The right document can help you access interviews and get you noticed. Alternative approaches to making useful contacts are also covered here.

State of mind

Now that you are ready to get going on the next phase, you need to check that you are in the right state of mind to do this properly. Applying for jobs is an assertive thing to do. In a sense you are selling yourself to potential employers who have thousands of pounds to pay you each year. In order to convince them that you are worth hiring, you need to believe it in spades yourself. Don't underestimate the power of an optimistic outlook. The time for feeling bitter or disappointed has gone. Now you have to concentrate on what you have to gain and what you have to offer. This is easier to say than to do, but just think if it were a friend who was starting their job search – you would be saying exactly the same to them.

This is the time to garner all the support you can. It can sometimes be easier to progress if you are in the company of people in the same position as yourself. You can make contacts through your local Jobcentre Plus office. Visit their central website at: www.jobcentreplus.gov.uk.

You can also download their Job Kit from this site, which contains useful advice and help for job seekers. There could be local job clubs in your area where you can work on your job search in conjunction with other people in exactly the same situation. If one doesn't exist in your area, why not start your own group, perhaps with ex-colleagues from your last workplace?

If you are feeling low, it can be difficult to think positively about your past achievements, particularly concerning the job from which you have just been made redundant. However from a potential employer's point of view, you need to put all that behind you now so that you can speak positively about what you can offer. The leaving of your last job is the least important thing about it. What you did there and your achievements are what matter. Your experience, skills and knowledge are what, combined, make the contribution you are able to offer to the next job.

Exercise

Spend a little time filling in the spaces below so that you bring that experience up to date. These questions are all those that you could be asked when applying for another job or training place.

My last job was as (position): . . . .

For (organization):. . . . .

My main tasks were:

_____

_____

_____

The skills I used were:

_____

_____

_____

My achievements were:

_____

_____

_____

I particularly enjoyed:

_____

_____

_____

What I learned there was:

_____

_____

_____

This gives you a starting point for describing and discussing your last role with future employers – something that can feel difficult after redundancy. Look at what you have written. How upbeat does it sound? Perhaps you could redo it, making the entries fuller and wording it more positively.

Take action!

Make sure your feelings about leaving your last job do not prejudice your description of what you did there.

You can use the exercise above for all your recent jobs. Then you will be thoroughly prepared for any kind of question about any of them.

Work–life balance

If you are ready to tackle looking for work again then you need to have the rest of your life organized to support you. Looking for work is a major activity in itself and you need the resources to do it properly. If there are people at home with you, talk through exactly what you are going to be doing over the next period to get their understanding. Explain to them that you may be a bit up and down, and enlist their support for the time, space and resources you will need for this activity.

You could do with a quiet place to work too. You will need to be engaged in thinking, reading and composing material so a space you can call your own, with a computer if possible, would be perfect. If you are struggling with space, motivation and facilities, a local job club may help to provide the resources you need.

It may be that you have altered the pattern of your life since redundancy, getting used to having more time for leisure and domestic issues. You now need to reclaim that space for work-related matters.

Thinking about the way forward might mean a readjustment between work and the rest of your life. Assessing yourself to see how balanced your life is now can be instructive. To evaluate this, complete the following questions:

1a)   What did you enjoy about your last job by the time you left?

1b)   What did you enjoy about your job initially?

2a)   What do you enjoy in your leisure time now?

2b)   What have you enjoyed in your leisure time previously?

3a)   Can you detect any patterns or recurring themes?

3b)   How can you do more to maximize the parts you like best?

Enjoyment is a powerful motivator at work as well as leisure. It is often the way we learn and remember best. Can you think of ways for the future to build more fun into your daily routine? Limited time requires good organization, high motivation and a goal-focused approach. If there are small tasks that you know need doing at some point, don't put them off.

Achieving balance in your life is a serious issue. How you live and work can affect your health and relationships. It forms a large part of how you perceive yourself and the values you hold to be important. Stress levels are much higher in manual workers, who have restricted choice over how they operate and achieve results. We work best when we have a clear idea of the purpose of our jobs and choice over the means to achieve it.

If there is just no place for passion, creativity and dreams at work, but expediency demands that we carry on with similar work, then we need to find other outlets for these in social and leisure activities. You can't always get everything you would like. Work commitments when younger (extensive travelling, long hours etc) may not be acceptable as we get older, have families or act as carers.

Consider keeping a job-search log of your activities. You can include what you are doing in other areas of your life too, or this could all be part of your daily diary. If you keep a track of what you are doing and spending time on, you may spot patterns that can be helpful. It may be that you do a better application form after a day that included some exercise, or that you have a more productive interview after spending the weekend with some friends who energized you with their company. All these pointers can be helpful in giving you new direction.

Take action!

Whatever needs doing, do it and do it now.

Preparing a CV

A CV (or curriculum vitae) is a document that tells the story of your life. It lists the jobs you have had and your educational achievements, as well as your skills and your interests. It may be a long time since you prepared a CV, if you have ever done so. CVs are often requested when jobs are advertised, and it is a very useful record to have as it provides an easy way to apply for jobs in the first instance. The key point about creating a successful CV is that it has to have greater impact than those of other people. It needs to include statements that differentiate yours from the other CVs in the pile on the employer's desk.

If you have not got an up-to-date CV, it may feel like a big challenge to know how to put this document together. It is quite common to feel that you can't remember what on earth you have done in your career. Dig out old CVs if you have them, or retrieve old copies of application forms that you have kept. Diaries and photographs may help you to piece together the story of your past. Call on the memories of people around you to help you put everything in order, so that you are ready to start on your document. You may well need to do several drafts of your CV so don't worry about making it perfect at the first attempt.

The helpful aspect of this document is that you are in charge of what you put in it. Unlike an application form where you have to complete the boxes provided for you, in your CV you can decide what you put in, how that is expressed and how you lay it out. This gives you more control, which is always helpful.

Here are the headings you need to complete as you start to compile your CV:

- Personal details:
  Name;
  Address;
  Postcode;
  Phone number;
  Mobile number;
  E-mail address.

- Education:
  In date order, including any exam passes from GCSE onwards.

- Employment history:
  Last job first, including place and type of work and main duties/achievements.

■ Other skills:
Practical knowledge.

■ Interests:
Spare time activities and hobbies.

■ Additional information/personal profile.

■ Referees:
Names of people to contact and their details.

Now let's take each of these headings in turn to check what
needs to be included in each one.

Personal details

■ Name: Put the full, formal name by which you are known
and how you would like to be addressed by your new
boss, so no pet names or middle names need appear here.

■ Address: This is your full, correct postal address including
the postal code.

■ Phone number: Your landline where you can be contacted
and messages can be left for you if you have one.

■ Mobile number: If you have one, full number where you
can be reached. You need to have either a landline or a
mobile number for your CV as an employer or recruitment
agency may well want to contact you by telephone if an
interview opportunity comes up. Make sure you have a
sensible and clear answerphone or voicemail message to
greet potential employers.

■ E-mail address: (If you have one, for electronic mail).

Education

(In date order, including any exam passes from GCSE onwards.)

In this section of your CV, the important aspects are the place at which you studied, the dates, title and main elements of the course and any exam passes you achieved.
   Example:

2009–2010	Powles Upper School Dulwich Hamlet London SE34	**GCSEs:** English Language, English Literature, Mathematics, Combined Science, History, Design Technology, Art

Writing in columns is the easiest way to depict this information. Start with your earliest studies and end with the most recent. Put the level of any qualification in bold type.

Employment history

(Last job first, including place and type of work and main duties/achievements.)

This section is for you to write down all the experience you have gained from different jobs.
   You need the dates, brief details of each employer, job title and an explanation of what you did plus any achievements while you were there.

Exercise

Use this table to collect together and write down your experience from different jobs. Concentrate on listing your main activities and the key part you played in each job. You could

make use of the exercise in the last chapter on page 109 to
generate some ideas for this table.

Dates	Place and location	Job title and key job areas and achievements

Using the layout shown in the table, fit these details into columns and edit what you are putting into each part to make
the impact of your experience as punchy as possible.

Example:

| 2007– 2010 | Barker's Pianos Birmingham B3 | **Sales Executive:** answering customers' queries; taking payments; stock checking; compiling product knowledge; briefing staff; arranging showroom; after-sales support.

Achieved the 'most successful branch' award for the last three years; regularly won team incentive prize for sales and service. |
|---|---|---|

The details describing each job need to illustrate the transferable skills that you have to offer, together with showing
any achievements that you contributed to your last job. The

skills that apply to both your previous jobs and the one for which you are applying show that you will bring a collection of abilities with you that can easily and quickly be used in the new role. The achievements give a flavour of the kind of benefit you will be able to contribute if you were to be employed by the new company. These are the key features that employers are looking for.

Quite often people leave without working out notice periods after redundancy. Even if you have left your organization you can still list yourself as employed there until you stop being paid by them.

Other skills

(Practical knowledge or skills of other kinds.)

Under this heading you can include other talents. These could include language ability, health and/or safety certificates, IT skills, driving ability or special licences – in fact anything you know about that doesn't fit anywhere else.

Interests

(Spare time activities and hobbies.)

Employers are interested in your spare-time interests. It shows a different side of you and enables you to include a variety of interests to show you enjoy something active, using your brain, something practical and something different. Cast your mind back to activities you used to spend time on or things that you used to do when you were at school or college.

Example:

I watch a lot of foreign language films and play netball locally once a week. I have just started learning the flute recently and

I enjoy playing for friends and family. I help to set and run quizzes for my local pub teams.

Additional information/personal profile

This section is to describe you as a person. It can include what you are offering an employer as well as details of any achievements from your working life.

This section can be a difficult one to write because it involves you 'selling yourself' by putting your strengths and your achievements to the fore. We are not used to puffing ourselves up in this way. This gets to the heart of the job-search process where making the most of yourself is key.

Write down six aspects of your personality that you think would be attractive to an employer.

1. _____

2. _____

3. _____

4. _____

5. _____

6. _____

Now turn these words or phrases into a couple of paragraphs that you can use to promote yourself in this section.

Example:

1. Quick learner.

2. Likes change.

3. Enjoy working in groups.

4. Results orientated.

5. Good at detail.

6. Motivator.

This list was turned into this passage:

> I am a quick learner who enjoys the challenge of implementing change. I am used to working in big groups to fulfil the aims set for us. Variety is important to me and I am able to keep focused on the bigger picture whilst finding my way through different short-term tasks. Attention to detail is one of my strengths, along with the ability to motivate and innovate.

Here is another example:

1. Ambitious.

2. Creative.

3. Learning new skills/knowledge.

4. Passionate.

5. Enthusiastic.

6. Committed.

The following paragraphs were constructed from this list:

> A hardworking, motivated and ambitious individual, my ambition and passion for professional development have seen me excel in both employment and academic studies, where I obtained a distinction. I am a team player and enjoy collaborating with colleagues, sharing knowledge and learning from others.
>
> My determination to do well and my creativity can be seen in my projects. I am a person of high integrity, a fast learner and my commitment to my work has seen me meet project deadlines whilst working under pressure. I strive to be the best

that I can be, and in doing so, bring only the utmost quality and professionalism to my work.

This part of your CV can either come at the front of the document to introduce yourself, or nearer the end to sum up the contribution you can make. It can be written in the first person as in the example above or in the third person, about you:

> Joel is a quick learner who enjoys the challenge of implementing change. He is used to working in big groups to fulfil their set aims. He thrives on variety and always keeps focused on the bigger picture whilst finding his way through different short-term tasks. Attention to detail is one of Joel's strengths, along with the ability to motivate and innovate.

You can choose which particular style appeals to you more and which you would be more comfortable using.

Referees

(Names of people to contact and their details.)

You need two people who can provide details of your character and work record. If possible one should be your last employer. Include their name, job position, e-mail and postal addresses. Make sure you ask their permission before including their names on your CV, and if a really important job is coming up, tell them all about it before they are approached for a reference.

Once you have written your CV in draft form, you need to convert it into the final version. Work through this checklist to move this process closer to a finished document.

- Lose the items that don't add anything to the overall impression.

- Get rid of details but make sure your transferable skills stand out.

- Correct the spelling and grammar.

- Beef up the language to use more active verbs and stronger descriptions.

- Look through the document to see its overall effect.

- Show the CV to trusted friends for their feedback.

CV presentation

The way your document looks is almost as important as what goes in it. You must spend time considering the way your CV will be read and viewed. This does not mean you need to go over the top with fancy fonts and elaborate display. On the contrary, keep it simple when you lay out the CV for the final version. A busy, fussy, over-complicated presentation will only put people off reading it. Just use bold or a slightly larger type to highlight your name, level of qualifications and job titles, then if your CV is looked at briefly, those vital points will stand out.

Use columns for your education and employment history if you can, to allow the reader's eye to scan the page easily and quickly. Writing in brief notes (or bullet points) when you have a list of items can save space and encourage a snappier feel to the document. Length is important. You need to keep this creation down to two or three pages maximum.

If you are sending a hard copy of your CV to an employer or a recruitment agency, use a heavier weight paper of at least 100 gms. Use only cream or white paper as it may be photocopied later on.

Alternative approaches

Having a CV that you can e-mail or send to employers is not the only way to start your job-search preparations.

Word of mouth is a powerful way to spread the news that you are available for work. It is still the case that many jobs are never advertised. If employers, particularly smaller ones, hear of a friend of an employee who wants a job, it may be easy to be taken on without a formal application procedure. So tell people you know and trust about your situation. Find a line to take, a way of describing your position.

'I am available for work now.'
'If you hear of any suitable job vacancies, I would be glad to know about them.'
'Do bear me in mind if any jobs come up at your place.'
'Let me know if you hear of any opportunities for work. I've got my CV ready.'

Social networking sites such as www.facebook.com allow you to advertise your availability to people you know and to increase your contacts. This could be an avenue to help you locate vacancies. On your Facebook page you can leave updates to say what you are doing, which could be a way to involve people in to your current situation. You could let people know what kind of work you would be interested in and how your job search is going. Be careful that you sound positive and upbeat though, not a sad loser, so talk about what is going well and your plans.

Electronic messaging such as Twitter enables you to talk to many people at once. If you have worked out a line you feel comfortable with, you could use this avenue to send out your message about being available for work. Don't forget that all your e-mail contacts and phone links are also available for you to work with.

Questions and answers

Q. My CV is over four pages long but I need that much space to do full justice to my career. Does this really matter?

A. Most CVs are under three pages long and the risk you take is that it may not be read at all if it is longer. Be ruthless in shortening it. Group employers together if they are of the same type, and use bullet points instead of full sentences. Cut down on the detail about your jobs to only include those items that are totally relevant to vacancies you are applying for, and preferably not from too long ago. If you feel there are projects, achievements or particularly significant work episodes from say, over 10 years ago, you can include them but only as long as you are sure that they definitely add a different element to the CV. Each point you include should add some new evidence about your worth. Concentrate on the key skills that you are offering and check that you are not duplicating any information.

Q. I get demoralized when I draft my CV as I can't get away from the fact that I have been made redundant and I am sure that will put future employers off. I have had a couple of temporary jobs but they don't look good on my CV as it is obvious I took them just as a way to earn some money.

A. As far as your recent work history goes, you can be proud of the fact that you are showing you are employable and resourceful, two of the concerns that employers could otherwise have. You can surely make some capital out of your present temporary jobs. Try and establish any connection you can between them and the vacancies you are applying for. Are customers or clients involved in the work? Have you learnt from any good or bad practice that you have seen? Are the systems well organized and the management effective? What is the atmosphere in these workplaces like? How could it be improved? Try and draw insights and learning points from wherever you are that could be useful for any future job.

With regard to your redundancy, the answer is to not let the leaving of your last job be the final word on your CV. Show that your short-term jobs are not all there is to you by finding other new elements to be able to write about: Register for evening classes, sign up for a charity fun run, learn a new skill, join in with a local volunteer scheme planting bulbs in the local park or reading to children in hospital. Do something right now to create a new present that totally overshadows the recent past and points to the many ways that you will contribute in your next and future roles.

Key points

1. Be clear what you can contribute to an employer.

2. Get in the right frame of mind to speak up for yourself.

3. A CV is a vital job-search tool.

4. You will benefit from time spent on the appearance of your CV.

5. Social networking can prove a helpful addition to your contacts.

9

Conducting a job search

Now you can start to accelerate your job-search techniques. Networking, once understood, is a powerful method of enlarging your search. Applying for vacancies needs careful organization. Online applications are more common now and have some specific dos and don'ts. Many selection processes use tests for applicants to assess abilities and knowledge relative to the job. There is specific preparation that you can undertake to get ready for this kind of test.

In this chapter you will find techniques to give you a better chance at your job interview. The advice it contains is relevant to people with a wide range of experience. Whatever your expertise or the level of job for which you are applying, using the tips and advice included here will help you to make more of an impact.

Being made redundant means that you suddenly have to start a job search when you may not have made any preparation for doing so and it may have been some time since you were in the job market.

Networking

You have lots of contacts in your life. When you are looking for work you can use these contacts to find out about job vacancies, get information about different types of work and spread the word about your search for work.

It may make you feel awkward and clumsy to have to 'use' friends in a very formal way. We are used to relating to people because we like them, not because we hope they can do something for us. However, you would not be annoyed or offended if a friend or ex-colleague of yours asked you for information about the kind of work you do, or to keep your eyes open for any vacancies. It is a truth that many jobs get filled through this kind of word-of-mouth recommendation. You do not want to miss the chance to get your next job that way. Similarly if you are called for an interview and want to find out more about the kind of work involved, you may realize that you have contacts who could provide you with valuable information on a job that they know about.

Start by thinking about who you know. You know many more people than you realize. Look through your address book to review contacts from the past. Take a little while to think about all the people you have come into contact with. Make a start to list them here:

- your network;
- education, schools and colleges;
- places of work;
- community organizations;

- neighbours;
- friends;
- family.

Then there are the friends of these friends that you have listed. You can see how the list can grow and grow. To construct your full list, you need to comb your e-mail address list, address book and phone list. Some of the people may be useful to you, or may know someone who could be.

Take action!

Making contact with two people each week from your network could help you find out about job vacancies.

Applying for vacancies

Many jobs are filled by the more typical route of filling in an application form. If you look for jobs in a national newspaper such as The *Guardian*, most of the vacancies ask for an application form as the method of applying for jobs advertised there. Forms can be sent to you in the post, downloaded from the company's website or filled in and returned electronically.

In essence all application forms are the same. They ask for your personal details, name, address, e-mail and phone numbers for contact purposes. They want full details of your education and training and your employment experience, including the knowledge that you have that will be transferable to the job on offer. They also want to know about your interests and any other skills that you may have. They finish with asking for details of two people who can provide character references for you. This is to show that you are worthy of employment and telling the truth about yourself.

Application forms are more common than CVs as a method of applying for jobs because employers can easily compare and contrast different forms and use computerized systems to sort and sift them, speeding up the selection process. So although the questions for each application form may look similar and straightforward, the expectations of the recipient may well be quite different. This means you can't just dash off an application form and expect it to get you an interview. Their completion is not just a formality. It requires planning, thought and detailed tailoring to fit the vacancy for each form you complete.

There are several crucial points in relation to application forms:

■ You must make sure to show exactly how you fit all the criteria specified by the employer in the details that you have been sent or have downloaded. Before filling in the form, analyse what the employer is asking for by carefully scrutinizing the job description and the person specification if you were sent them.

■ Check out the employer's website for more clues about what they want. Just because you are familiar with a part-icular type of work, that doesn't mean you will pitch your application correctly unless you research all you can about the organization. Its website or written communications can provide you with a wealth of information about its outlook, priorities and vision for the future.

■ Look for 'key words', or short phrases that crop up fre-quently in terms of skills, knowledge or levels of respons-ibility. These words could be used to screen for the first shortlist of candidates to interview because the employer does not want to see anyone who does not have a basic set of skills for the job. Examples of such words could be: 'technical, supervisory, team player, account executive, creative, manager'. Or there could be a type of work that is screened for, such as 'project, databases, programming, IT, Excel'.

Describing your redundancy

A critical issue after redundancy is how you describe your recent history on any form you complete. Obviously redundancy can happen to anyone at any time and employers understand that. After redundancy, a frequently asked question is: 'How will an employer react when they see that I have been made redundant?'

The answer to this important question is that employers will start from a neutral position and will then be strongly influenced by the way that you pitch the story about yourself. If you see your redundancy as being a massive personal blow that has stopped your career in its tracks and devastated all your plans, the employer is likely to see your situation in that light too.

If, however, you project yourself as taking this change of plans in your stride, seeing it as all part of life's rich tapestry and realizing that it was the role that was made redundant, not you; if you show that you see this as a temporary hiatus not a permanent disaster, the employer is much more likely to perceive your situation in the same way.

If you can go one step further and demonstrate that, far from stalling your career, you are using this as an opportunity to move ahead in a different way now, learning as you go and using every possibility to develop, reflect and contribute, you could be seen as a great potential asset. The image you want to create is that everything in your life has been leading up to this point today. You are available with all your skills and knowledge, experience and personality, ready to make a terrific contribution if the employer is wise and quick enough to offer you the job.

So, to turn the question back on itself: 'How are you planning to describe your current situation to an employer?'

Now, what if you left your last job a while ago, perhaps not having been lucky in finding a job, or you took some time off to travel or pursue an interest? How might this be judged by a potential employer?

Always think about this from a potential employer's point of view. What doubts might they have about an application form that tells this story? They may worry that you are not a good candidate for employment because you have not been successful in getting a job so far. They may think that you could be out of touch or that your skills may be rusty. They may wonder if you were just wasting your time when you were on your travels rather than building up your life experience.

The answer is in your hands, because the challenge is to demonstrate from all the things that you have been spending time on that you have used them to enhance your employability. For instance, if you have been travelling you will have seen other cultures; perhaps you took the chance to learn a little of new languages; you will have been flexible and adaptable and improved your communication skills; you may have made new contacts and experienced other ways of working and doing business. You need to always be thinking about how you can use what you have done to demonstrate to a future employer how all this adds to the contribution that you can bring.

Almost everyone who applies will fit the minimum specified by the job description. On its own that will not be enough. Your application has to be brighter and better than others. I have known excellent candidates passed over at the application stage because their forms were just not interesting enough to make them stand out. At a recent interview, a candidate dropped out and the next-best applicant was called in to take his place. This candidate had not been selected initially because her application seemed to provide nothing particularly special. She was excellent at the interview and got the job, but it was only due to the absence of the first choice that she was interviewed. On the strength of her application form alone, she had been passed over and put on the reject list.

So don't just dash off application forms. Quality, not quantity is what will win through. If you rush a form, it won't impress anyone. You need to take time over what you are writing so that it is tailored properly to the vacancy and that you make the most of yourself. A priority is describing your situation positively. Use bold adjectives to highlight your strengths and achievements, show your enthusiasm through the tone you set in your paperwork. It will all contribute to the impression you make with the recruiter.

Online applications

Increasingly, employers and recruitment agencies are asking for applications to be filled in and then e-mailed, or completed online. This makes the process quicker and more streamlined for them. All the applications received can be easily analysed and processed but this way of dispatching forms can present some dangers for the job seeker.

Filling in online applications also needs careful attention to the use of key words as they will often be used to filter out unwanted applications at the first stage. Make sure you fill in the boxes to any word limit set and be careful about your presentation. You cannot retrieve a form once you have sent it in.

Do not make any mistakes on the form. It is all too easy to press 'Send' in a fit of enthusiasm just to find errors afterwards. Never send a form without printing it out to proofread it first. Somehow it is more difficult to see typing mistakes on the screen. Leave the form for a couple of hours, then return to it to check it through.

Preparing for selection tests

With a lot of candidates applying for every job, the majority of whom would be capable of doing the job, many employers use selection tests to filter out the best from the rest. They try to use only tests that are relevant to the job they are advertising, so you should not worry about being hit by a topic you know nothing about. You should not find any test terribly difficult if it is a job you are suited to.

These tests can take many forms and you may find several types being used together. Ability or attainment tests look at what you know on the day of the test. Some are concerned with your general aptitude or capacity to do a job. This may include your attitude to and suitability to the subject as well as your current knowledge.

These are the main types of area tested:

- Verbal reasoning:
  These tests are concerned with checking your ability with words and understanding.

- Numerical ability:
  These are tests of ability, speed and accuracy with number problems. Numerical reasoning tests see if you can pick out the key points shown by numerical tables etc.

Written tests

These show your skills in a professional area such as composing a press release, or test your writing ability such as drafting a letter to a customer.

In-tray exercise

Here you are given a series of tasks that could face you in your job and asked to put them in priority order and say how you would deal with them. An example could be an exercise for a senior manager: the items to be dealt with could include a letter from the CEO to a business partner that has to be drafted, a memo on a personnel dispute that needs writing as it is just about to blow up, a staff away-day to be planned and fire procedures to be posted on the staff intranet. You will be marked on an exercise like this in terms of the priorities you give tasks as well as how you execute them.

Psychometric tests

For more senior positions, you could be asked to complete a battery of psychometric tests. These assess your personality, competence and abilities in different spheres depending on the job. The resulting assessment comes in the form of a report on the different areas, providing a summary of your suitability for the post. If you are able to see the results, they can provide interesting reading about the way the test saw you. You could find useful pointers for your future career even if you did not get the job.

Group discussions

Some employers arrange a formal discussion with staff or other candidates to assess how you perform as part of a group. This could assess your personal manner and confidence and your ability to bring people into the discussion, as well as your answers to the set questions.

Practising ability tests can boost your results. Being used to the type of questions that you will face takes away some of the strangeness of the experience, and there is a definite knack of how to approach the different types of questions. You will boost your chances if you read up about this topic in a book with practice examples for you to work on. There are many helpful titles on selection tests. At the end of this book, on page 162, you will find a list of those published by Kogan Page that can help you with this subject.

Interview techniques

Most jobs are filled using a job interview. This is where you are invited in to meet the employer and to tell them about yourself. Sometimes you will be asked to give a presentation on some aspect of the job at the same time. Normally you will be asked questions about yourself, your background and about how you see the job in question.

Interviews can be a daunting prospect but you need to jump this hurdle in order to get the job. They therefore also represent a terrific opportunity, and if you are called for an interview you are doing very well. It means that the application you have submitted has interested the employer. If you had been in the same job for a long period, you may not have had an interview for some years. Don't panic!

The main thing is to enjoy the experience and to treat it as an opportunity to describe yourself fully to the employer. The people who fail at interview often simply don't make the most of themselves. They could do the job but fail to impress the panel with their answers. They don't speak up enough about what they know, what they can do and their ideas for the job.

The range of questions could cover any of the following areas:

▧ School and college experience: what you did there and why you chose those courses, what you learned and what skills and knowledge it left you with.

▧ Employment history: different jobs you have done, achievements and successes, what you have learned, difficulties and challenges, why you left your last job, examples of projects you have worked on.

▧ General: equal opportunities.

▧ Interests: what hobbies you have, links to any of your jobs, evidence of a rounded personality.

▧ Your personality: your outlook, what sort of a person you are, likes and dislikes, strengths and weaknesses, your ambitions and career plans.

▧ The job: your vision for the job, how you would do the job, what contribution will you make to it, what you see as the main tasks.

▧ The employer: what you know about the organization, why you are applying.

For each question try and prepare three key points that you can convey in your answer.

Example:

Q1. Why do you want to work for this organization?
     Three key points: relevant experience; right set of skills; personality would fit.

A.   I have experience in this sort of work. I spent four years with Belton Brothers on the sales floor – work I enjoyed. During that period I covered all the different products and became a bit of an expert on the stock. Colleagues were always asking my advice for customers. Knowing a lot about the products means that you can be extra helpful to the customers, and providing the best service to them is the most important part of the job to me. This is exactly the job where I could make a real contribution as a keen and motivated team player.

Q2.   What is your vision for the job?
Three key points: build on good practice; introduce new ideas; form a strong team.

A.   I am sure there is a lot of excellent work going on in the design department already and I would spend my first weeks getting to know all about that and the people who work here. One of the benefits of coming in to a new place is being able to introduce new ideas. In my last company we recently worked on some innovative ways of liaising with our clients, which improved the satisfaction results enormously: I would be keen to introduce that innovation here. Mainly I know that together with the existing staff here, I will be able to forge a new team to raise the profile of the firm even higher in this competitive sector.

Take action!

For each interview answer you prepare, include a concrete example or illustration so that the employer can imagine you doing the job for real.

Talking about your situation

It is highly likely that you will be asked questions that specifically relate to your redundancy. Here are some examples:

Tell us how you came to leave your last job.
Why did you leave your last position?
How did your last employment end?

You need to have a ready answer prepared for this question. Why would an employer ask this question? They want an explanation of why you left your last job, they are interested in getting reassurance that you did not have any particular problem there and they want to know how you feel about your last employer.

Once we know this, it can help us to frame an answer.

Your three key points could be: post made redundant; sad to go; good relations.

Your answer could go something like:

The company reorganized earlier this year because of falling income. My post was one of 15 made redundant from the head office. I was sad to leave as I had enjoyed my three years there, although I quite understood the necessity to restructure at that time. I am still in touch with ex-colleagues and left on very good terms with everyone.

Other questions may be about what you have been doing since you left:

How have you spent your time since you left your last post?
Have you been applying for lots of jobs?

What is behind asking this kind of question? The employer wants to know that you have used your time productively, that you are employable and that you see this particular vacancy as a significant one.

Your three key points could be: spent time productively; have had fill-in jobs; contribution to this particular post.

Your answer could go:

> I didn't want to rush into just any job so I took some temping work to tide me over. It has been a useful period as I have had new experiences to add to my CV and have seen a different side of the retail business by working on the shop floor. I could see this would be valuable, and when the job with you came up, I knew it could be the perfect opportunity for me to use all my experience to make a major contribution to your sales office.

You may even get provocative questions like:

> You left your last job a while ago. What have you been doing in the meantime?

Don't be tempted to look back too much and dwell on what came before, as it can leave an impression of someone who is a bit stuck in the past.

Your three key points could be: choosing what to do carefully; happy with where I am now; have got a lot to offer.

Your answer might include:

> I wanted to make the right choice of my next proper job. My time has been filled productively, helping a local allotment committee to get organized. I have extensive skills and knowledge in accountancy and this coupled with my communication skills and values, means that I have a lot to offer a company where I really 'fit'.

You need to sound upbeat but without sounding as though you are just glossing over everything. Pull out positive features concerning things you have learnt or contributed to show how you would continue to do this in a new role.

You could be asked:

What's your view of your last company now?

Resist going into too much detail about the redundancy but try and give credit for anything that was handled well.

These could perhaps be your three points: difficult situation; tried to protect staff; wish them well.

Your answer could go:

> Any redundancy programme is bound to be difficult for everyone involved. The organization tried to lay people off as fairly as possible. I got caught because I hadn't been there long. Looking back it was well handled, with the longest-serving staff protected. I hope they manage to survive now they are a leaner organization, even if I will be making my own contribution elsewhere.

Researching all you can about the new company is vital before your interview. Find out everything you can about the organization, its vision and products and services. You will be expected to talk about these things and show how well you could fit into the team. It is not enough just to be familiar with your own CV and background.

The most crucial area for your preparation is in answering the question about why you want the job. Often people are scared of answering this one but it is the perfect opportunity to tell the employer exactly what you are offering. This should include your skills and knowledge, your experience and your personality. If you can include information about how you would do the job and where you see the organization going with your help, so much the better.

Doing a presentation

Being asked to give a presentation on an aspect of the job concerned can be seen as a type of test. This shows your confidence, ability to speak in public and your command of the topic set. You are often given the subject before the day of the interview, but you may only be set it on the day of the interview itself. If this is the case you will have preparation time as part of the interview. You can do a lot of work in advance to think about possible questions that could come up, just by using the materials that the employer has sent you and your common sense.

Take action!

Practise your interview presentation out loud to rehearse it.

Questions and answers

Q. I don't have anything new to wear to an interview and no money to buy a new suit. Will this count against me?

A. No. Employers are not going to look in detail at your clothes. You only need to look smart, clean and as though you have tried hard to prepare for this important occasion. The two essentials are proper shoes (not sandals or trainers) and a formal top. Even if you don't have a suit, can you get hold of a smart jacket in a dark colour? Beg or borrow one from a friend or member of your family. You will need a white or light top or shirt underneath it. Wear plain coloured clothes and make sure your hair is washed and shoes cleaned. If you are receiving Jobseeker's

Allowance you may be entitled to a clothing grant to assist you attending interviews. Take a look at the website www.direct.gov.uk for more details.

Q. How do I combat nerves? Since my redundancy I am a gibbering wreck in interviews.

A. First, before you enter the room, form the vowel sounds with your mouth, but say them silently, stretching your mouth very wide in all directions as you do so 'aaaaa, eeeee, iiiii, ooooo, uuuuu'. You will look ridiculous so make sure that no one can see you. This will limber up the muscles around the mouth to help you enunciate clearly. Second, smile when you enter the room. The panel will smile back at you and that helps a lot. Third, and most importantly, breathe. If you find that everything is going blank and you are losing your way, pause, breathe two or three times, then you will feel your head clearing and you will be able to continue. All nerves are a product of lack of oxygen, so this breathing tip is a vital remedy to use when the nerves hit you.

Remember though that every single interview candidate suffers from nerves so you are not alone, and panels make allowances for this.

Key points

1. Everyone feels nervous trying to get a new job. Don't let this hold you back.

2. Almost everyone who is in work has had to get over the hurdle of applications and interviews, so just get going.

3. The employer will need to know what special contribution you can bring to the organization. Are you clear what that is?

4. Use your contacts to get information that will give you the advantage.

5. Keep well organized in your job search. Copies of all your paperwork will come in handy when attending interviews or applying for similar jobs later on.

10

Self-employment

Many of us put together a portfolio career made up of different types of work. We may spend some time working for ourselves and some in paid employment. As you consider your future, it could be worth thinking through the other income generators that could be open to you.

Self-employment is a great option for some people. You need to decide whether it is for you. Some people make a living out of consultancy, and several examples are given in this chapter of this kind of work. Freelance work generally can throw up new issues to consider and these are covered here.

A portfolio career

A portfolio career is the term given to one that is made up of several different components. Janet is a good example. She works from home as a journalist, writing articles commissioned individually by different women's magazines, for part of each week. In addition she runs a Pilates class at the local leisure centre twice a week and also does some proofreading for a publishing house. Her week is made up of this patchwork of three discrete job areas, all of which contribute to the income she needs to survive. She says this about her arrangement:

> The fact that I do all these bits and pieces of work spreads the risk of one income stream drying up completely. After I was made redundant from a major magazine two years ago, I decided not to put all my eggs in one basket again. This way, I won't get to be a millionaire but at least I feel a bit more secure that if one element goes pear-shaped, I can still earn a living.
>
> Also I could expand any one type of work if I had to. If the proofreading came to an end, I could always put on more Pilates classes or vice versa. I am up-to-date with three work areas so can change the proportions of each in my portfolio if I need to. The downside is that I have to be incredibly well organized to keep on top of it all but so far that has worked out OK.

Some people create a portfolio like this to cushion them against the vulnerability of full-time self-employment. You can build up your business whilst still being paid for part of each week.

John says:

> I am working as a music teacher part time at a local school as I am starting up my own teaching practice at home. At the moment I am doing three days a week in school but am planning to reduce that next year as my own business is doing quite well and I would rather move to a whole week with my pupils coming to me.

Other income generators

When you are trying to ensure you have an income to a certain level, it is worth trying to think as widely as you can about ways to increase your earning power. It might be the case that you can make money in other ways. Your labour may not be the only asset that you have. If you have your own property, you may want to think about letting out a spare room. Although this may not be part of your longer-term plan, it could be a way of easing the financial pressure in the short term.

James was made redundant from his job in a warehouse. He says:

> I decided to rent out a room in my house to keep me going. Both my boys had to sleep in the same room for a year but it gave me a basic level of income at a time when otherwise I was going to be worrying about money. My sons understood that our lifestyle had to change a bit and we had some fun decorating the room they both slept in, so that helped. It meant that I could take a job as a security guard at a lower salary, knowing that I was slightly protected by the rental income of £300 each month.

Even if you don't want a permanent lodger there could be other possibilities. Philippa was panicking about money:

> I heard that the local college needed places for foreign students for a few weeks. I had two Germans first. They shared a room that has two beds in it, I only had to provide breakfast for them and then they were out at college all day. As far as I was concerned it was an easy way of making some money and as it was only for a month it did not disrupt life in the house too much. I will definitely do it again.

Even if you don't have flexibility around your assets, you may be able to reduce your outgoings. Hard though it might be to consider, a car is a big expense. Perhaps you could live without one for a couple of years, particularly if you live in a town with effective public transport. Evaluate all of your outgoings to see if there are ways to shave expenditure just for the short term.

Self-employment, is it for you?

For some people, working for themselves is a good option. For others it could represent a nightmare. Here are the most common good and bad points. Take a long look at each list to evaluate how important each point seems to you.

Advantages

- Life is under your control.
- You are free.
- You are in charge.
- You have opportunities for creative endeavour.
- You can choose how to spend your time.
- You can organize your business the way you want to.
- You can work as much or as little as you want.
- You control the quality of what you provide.
- You get all the praise and bouquets.
- You could earn a lot of money.
- You might make your fortune.

- If you survive beyond three years you could do well in the long term.

- You can always get another job if it does not work out.

Disadvantages

- Making money may be difficult and it might be harder to equal your previous income.

- It can be lonely with no peer group or team for support.

- It can be hard to innovate alone.

- You are totally responsible and have to take full blame for what goes wrong.

- You may find that what sells is not what you want to provide.

- Starting up can use up all your resources.

- You need capital behind you to market the business.

- People who are good at making things or providing services are not necessarily business minded.

- You could end up in debt.

- Most new businesses fail within the first three years.

- It can take three to five years to make any money out of the business.

- It is much harder to get a mortgage when you only have self-employed income.

- There are no guarantees that you will make enough to live on.

- There is no sick pay, holiday pay, maternity leave, pension provision or any other perks unless you provide them.

■ It might be harder to get back into the job market after a long gap.

The weight you attach to each of the points above can help you decide whether to work for yourself or not. But before you commit yourself to self-employment it is worth thinking the pros and cons through with your family, particularly if you are the main wage earner. What might seem like a chance for freedom and the end of being a wage-slave to you could seem like a recipe for stress and conflict to your partner. If you are lucky enough to live with someone who is earning and who can maintain your income and support your lifestyle as you begin entry into self-employment, that could provide the perfect compromise.

There is plenty of information for those new to starting a business. See the government website www.businesslink.gov. uk, which is a very comprehensive site containing much of use including details of business grants and loans available.

Steps to self-employment

Finding your niche

What are you planning to provide or sell? Most people go into business because they have something specific that they are skilled at providing, making or offering. You may have spotted a need for this product or service, or you may think you can generate enough interest in the product through advertising and marketing.

Market research

What evidence do you have that there is a market for this product or service? You need to ask people what they want, how much they will pay and in what form they would expect to buy this product or service. Pricing decisions will need to be based on what the market will bear. What are your competitors charging?

This kind of research, even if conducted very informally, can give you clear pointers to what will work and can lower the risk of failure. You will find out what price you can charge, and understand what sort of volume you therefore need to sell to make a profit.

Getting customers

Many people are so carried away with the seductive picture of how well they are likely to do in their new business that they forget to budget for marketing it. It is very rare for a business to do well, however hardworking the owner, unless a substantial amount of money is invested in marketing. Potential customers need to be wooed to try out your offer, and then reminded to come back again.

Cash flow

Cash forecasts can help you predict the early path this business will take. Good advice is normally to start small and to restrict what you are spending until you know how the business is progressing.

Borrowing money to invest

Raising finance if it is necessary, will require a solid business plan to show how the business will grow and be successful. You may find small amounts can be raised from people you know, which can be helpful in the early days.

Business name and legal status

You can just be a sole trader without any fuss but if you want to register yourself as a business entity, you will need to have a registered name and full details of all the owners.

Premises

Paying for accommodation is expensive and best avoided if possible until you have done a lot of research to check what is needed and the best location in which to settle. Obviously some businesses, such as restaurants, need premises straight away but other services may allow you to work at home at least initially.

Money matters

Tax liability needs to be checked early in the life of a business so that the financial affairs are in order straight from the start to avoid any problems.

Employing people

Taking on staff is very expensive. Putting people on the payroll should only happen when there is evidence of enough demand to pay for them.

Use these factors to consider ways to form an outline business plan that you can then discuss with professional advisers. There are many helpful books that can give you useful information to help you prepare for running your own business. Look at the list of Kogan Page titles on page 162 for some titles on this subject.

Take action!

Get tips from a financial adviser before you commit to self-employment.

What is consultancy?

Consultancy is a form of self-employment providing expertise and specialist skills to a series of different employers, often at a management level. You are paid only for what you provide. Most consultants specialize in one sort of skill, such as project management, IT management or HR.

Freelance work

Freelance work is another variation on self-employment. As a freelancer you can provide all sorts of different services for sale, depending on the demand.

Franchises

Some people buy into an existing business on a self-employed basis. This can give you the security of working with the 'name' of an established organization whilst still being your own boss. Beware though of franchise operations inflating their predictions of what you may earn from the business and asking for large investments of cash to buy in to the franchise. Always get some independent advice before taking the plunge into being a franchisee.

Take action!

Talk to existing franchisees before handing money over for a franchise.

Issues to consider

As part of a career plan, being self-employed can seem like a big step to take but it could bring big rewards. Jake says:

> I started coaching when I was made redundant and haven't looked back. I hooked up with the local cricket club, who were very short of coaches. They gave me enough work to start me off and it has gone well ever since. In the winter I coach football in local schools. I couldn't be happier and it's all thanks to being laid off from my last job.

Sarah, a financial adviser to small businesses, says:

> Most people I advise are good at their craft, service or creative product, just hopeless at the business side. They normally wildly overestimate the income that they can bring in, seriously underestimate how much everything will cost and totally forget that to establish a customer base you need a lot of money to invest in marketing the business before anyone will come and buy.

Questions and answers

Q. I have decided to go freelance. Should I set up a website?

A. Yes. Most people would expect someone self-employed to have a presence on the web these days. Don't spend a lot of money on it though. Lots of people get overly concerned with business stationery, elaborate websites and complicated logos before they have even got one sale. Just create a single page so that people know what you are doing, they can contact you easily and you can link your site up with others in a similar field. You can always develop it to be all-singing and all-dancing at a later stage. The only other item of stationery you require is a business card to carry at all times.

Q. The isolation is what worries me. I am working for myself and find it difficult to keep inspired, and I haven't got time to be endlessly seeing friends.

A. Join a local business club or trade or professional association. They will all meet fairly regularly and you can combine social with business, making good contacts, learning about relevant issues whilst also meeting people in the same boat as yourself. Look for local groups through a search engine such as www.google.co.uk.

Key points

1. It can take a long time to build up a business from scratch.

2. Most people borrow money from a bank initially to set up in business.

3. Self-employment tends to suit self-reliant loners rather than team players.

4. Make sure you have all the insurances you need to set up in business.

5. Keep enough reserves so that you can weather cash-flow problems.

Conclusion

Now it is time to look to the future. You can start planning ahead for the next stage after redundancy. Auditing the resources open to you can help you to put a stronger plan together.

The next phase of your life does need to get going though, and the sooner you can start looking to the future the better. Most of us need to work to survive and by taking the first step now, your future will get established.

Putting it all together requires a positive mental attitude and a determination to keep on trying until you succeed. You are not out of work, you just have a different job or project to work on for the immediate future: finding your next job or deciding on your next career move, starting a business, building a portfolio, developing your retirement activities or some other idea.

The first step is to come to terms with what has happened to you. Even if you were happy to be made redundant, it can still come as quite a shock to find yourself out of work, especially if you have worked for the same employer for many years. It can be a severe blow if you did not welcome it. However, although it seems to loom very large in your life now, you will not be defined forever as that person who was made redundant. Many of us have been through this experience and come out satisfactorily at the other end. It will not wreck your life.

Then it is worthwhile to spend some time working out what you have to offer. Planning ahead can be very worthwhile. Thinking through what you want, what you need and what you can offer can help you establish exactly which option is most sensible and feasible at the present time. If as part of that you conduct an accurate resource audit, to see what you are spending, what assets you have and what skills and abilities too, you will be able to negotiate for your future with authority. You will know your worth.

When you start your job search, you know that you have good advice behind you and a clear outlook onto what you want and what contribution you are offering.

Use this book to develop your action plan. As you read through, complete the exercises to help you move forward. Plug into your networks and use the resources out there. Good luck!

Appendix 1: Statutory redundancy pay table

To use this table simply read across from your age at the date of redundancy shown in the left-hand column and down from your years of service at that date shown across the top of the table. For example someone who is 45 years old with 10 years' service would be entitled to 12 weeks' redundancy pay.

Statutory redundancy pay table

Age	Service (years)																		
	2	3	4	5	6	7	8	9	10	11	12	13	14	15	16	17	18	19	20
17	1																		
18	1	1½																	
19	1	1½	2																
20	1	1½	2	2½	–														
21	1	1½	2	2½	3	–													
22	1	1½	2	2½	3	3½	–												
23	1½	2	2½	3	3½	4	4½	–											
24	2	2½	3	3½	4	4½	5	5½	–										
25	2	3	3½	4	4½	5	5½	6	6½	–									
26	2	3	4	4½	5	5½	6	6½	7	7½	–								
27	2	3	4	5	5½	6	6½	7	7½	8	8½	–							
28	2	3	4	5	6	6½	7	7½	8	8½	9	9½	–						
29	2	3	4	5	6	7	7½	8	8½	9	9½	10	10½	–					
30	2	3	4	5	6	7	8	8½	9	9½	10	10½	11	11½	–				
31	2	3	4	5	6	7	8	9	9½	10	10½	11	11½	12	12½	–			
32	2	3	4	5	6	7	8	9	10	10½	11	11½	12	12½	13	13½	–		
33	2	3	4	5	6	7	8	9	10	11	11½	12	12½	13	13½	14	14½	–	
34	2	3	4	5	6	7	8	9	10	11	12	12½	13	13½	14	14½	15	15½	–
35	2	3	4	5	6	7	8	9	10	11	12	13	13½	14	14½	15	15½	16	16½
36	2	3	4	5	6	7	8	9	10	11	12	13	14	14½	15	15½	16	16½	17
37	2	3	4	5	6	7	8	9	10	11	12	13	14	15	15½	16	16½	17	17½
38	2	3	4	5	6	7	8	9	10	11	12	13	14	15	16	16½	17	17½	18

Statutory redundancy pay table

Age	Service (years)																		
	2	3	4	5	6	7	8	9	10	11	12	13	14	15	16	17	18	19	20
39	2	3	4	5	6	7	8	9	10	11	12	13	14	15	16	17	17½	18	18½
40	2	3	4	5	6	7	8	9	10	11	12	13	14	15	16	17	18	18½	19
41	2	3	4	5	6	7	8	9	10	11	12	13	14	15	16	17	18	19	19½
42	2½	3½	4½	5½	6½	7½	8½	9½	10½	11½	12½	13½	14½	15½	16½	17½	18½	19½	20½
43	3	4	5	6	7	8	9	10	11	12	13	14	15	16	17	18	19	20	21
44	3	4½	5½	6½	7½	8½	9½	10½	11½	12½	13½	14½	15½	16½	17½	18½	19½	20½	21½
45	3	4½	6	7	8	9	10	11	12	13	14	15	16	17	18	19	20	21	22
46	3	4½	6	7½	8½	9½	10½	11½	12½	13½	14½	15½	16½	17½	18½	19½	20½	21½	22½
47	3	4½	6	7½	9	10	11	12	13	14	15	16	17	18	19	20	21	22	23
48	3	4½	6	7½	9	10½	11½	12½	13½	14½	15½	16½	17½	18½	19½	20½	21½	22½	23½
49	3	4½	6	7½	9	10½	12	13	14	15	16	17	18	19	20	21	22	23	24
50	3	4½	6	7½	9	10½	12	13½	14½	15½	16½	17½	18½	19½	20½	21½	22½	23½	24½
51	3	4½	6	7½	9	10½	12	13½	15	16	17	18	19	20	21	22	23	24	25
52	3	4½	6	7½	9	10½	12	13½	15	16½	17½	18½	19½	20½	21½	22½	23½	24½	25½
53	3	4½	6	7½	9	10½	12	13½	15	16½	18	19	20	21	22	23	24	25	26
54	3	4½	6	7½	9	10½	12	13½	15	16½	18	19½	20½	21½	22½	23½	24½	25½	26½
55	3	4½	6	7½	9	10½	12	13½	15	16½	18	19½	21	22	23	24	25	26	27
56	3	4½	6	7½	9	10½	12	13½	15	16½	18	19½	21	22½	23½	24½	25½	26½	27½
57	3	4½	6	7½	9	10½	12	13½	15	16½	18	19½	21	22½	24	25	26	27	28
58	3	4½	6	7½	9	10½	12	13½	15	16½	18	19½	21	22½	24	25½	26½	27½	28½
59	3	4½	6	7½	9	10½	12	13½	15	16½	18	19½	21	22½	24	25½	27	28	29
60	3	4½	6	7½	9	10½	12	13½	15	16½	18	19½	21	22½	24	25½	27	28½	29½
61+	3	4½	6	7½	9	10½	12	13½	15	16½	18	19½	21	22½	24	25½	27	28½	30

Appendix 2: Useful contacts

Job search

www.jobcentreplus.gov.uk: a portal to all the Jobcentre Plus services.

www.prospects.ac.uk: the leading graduate careers website with advice and other resources.

www.facebook.com: a large social networking site.

www.jobs.guardian.co.uk: a newspaper website with the largest selection of vacancies.

www.timesonline.co.uk: the website for the Times newspaper group.

www.ft.com: the website for the *Financial Times*.

www.londonjobs.co.uk: the website of the *Evening Standard* newspaper in London.

www.fish4jobs.co.uk/iad/jobs: a website providing a summary of local newspapers' jobs.

www.reed.co.uk: a site owned by Reed, a large employment agency group.

www.jobsgopublic.com: a public sector and not-for-profit website.

www.jobs.co.uk: a site that searches other job boards for you.

www.monster.co.uk: a job-search site with many vacancies.

www.totaljobs.com: a job-search site with many vacancies.

Advice and information

www.careersadvice.direct.gov.uk: a government site offering free careers advice. Their helpline number is 0800 100 900.

www.connexions-direct.com/jobs4u: an excellent source of information about every job you could ever think of, with details of entry levels and qualifications needed, training courses, pay etc.

Education and training

www.learndirect-advice.co.uk: a government-funded service to provide advice about local opportunities and sources of help with learning and training. Their helpline number is 0800 101 901.

www.educationandtraining.org.uk: a site offering information on learning opportunities of all types.

The Open University: www.open.ac.uk.

Finances and self-employment

A government website, www.businesslink.gov.uk, is a very comprehensive site including details of business grants and loans available.

www.taxaid.org.uk is a charity providing free tax advice.

National debt helpline: 0808 808 4000; www.nationaldebtline. co.uk. Run by the Money Advice Trust, this is a confidential, free debt advice line available to everyone.

Volunteering

VSO www.vso.org.uk: an international development charity that works through volunteer placements.

REACH the skilled volunteering charity: www.volwork.org. uk.

www.do-it.org.uk and www.volunteering.org.uk: sites that enable you to search for voluntary opportunities in your locality.

www.thecareerbreaksite.com: a site for short-term volunteer opportunities.

Personal/health

NHS Direct: online at www.nhsdirect.nhs.uk, or call their helpline on 0845 4647.

The Samaritans: 08457 90 9090; www.samaritans.org, a helpline for those in distress or despair.

Mind: www.mind.org.uk, the mental health charity.

General

www.direct.gov.uk: the portal for all government services in the UK.

Further reading from Kogan Page

Advanced IQ Tests
ISBN 978 0 7494 5232 2
The Advanced Numeracy Test Workbook
ISBN 978 0 7494 5406 7
Aptitude, Personality & Motivation Tests
ISBN 978 0 7494 5651 1
The Aptitude Test Workbook
ISBN 978 0 7494 5237 7
A-Z of Careers & Jobs
ISBN 978 0 7494 5510 1
Careers After the Armed Forces
ISBN 978 0 7494 5530 9
Career, Aptitude & Selection Tests
ISBN 978 0 7494 5695 5
Graduate Psychometric Test Workbook
ISBN 978 0 7494 5405 0

Great Answers to Tough Interview Questions
ISBN 978 0 7494 5196 7
How to Master Nursing Calculations
ISBN 978 0 7494 5162 2
How to Master Psychometric Tests
ISBN 978 0 7494 5165 3
How to Pass Advanced Aptitude Tests
ISBN 978 0 7494 5236 0
How to Pass Advanced Numeracy Tests
ISBN 978 0 7494 5229 2
How to Pass Advanced Verbal Reasoning Tests
ISBN 978 0 7494 4969 8
How to Pass the Civil Service Qualifying Tests
ISBN 978 0 7494 4853 0
How to Pass Data Interpretation Tests
ISBN 978 0 7494 4970 4
How to Pass Diagrammatic Reasoning Tests
ISBN 978 0 7494 4971 1
How to Pass the BMAT
ISBN 978 0 7494 5461 6
How to Pass the GMAT
ISBN 978 0 7494 4459 4
How to Pass Graduate Psychometric Tests
ISBN 978 0 7494 4852 3
How to Pass Numeracy Tests
ISBN 978 0 7494 5706 8
How to Pass Numerical Reasoning Tests
ISBN 978 0 7494 4796 0
How to Pass the Police Selection System
ISBN 978 0 7494 5712 9
How to Pass Professional Level Psychometric Tests
ISBN 978 0 7494 4207 1
How to Pass the QTS Numeracy Skills Test
ISBN 978 0 7494 5460 9
How to Pass Selection Tests
ISBN 978 0 7494 5693 1

How to Pass Technical Selection Tests
ISBN 978 0 7494 4375 7
How to Pass the UKCAT
ISBN 978 0 7494 5333 6
How to Pass the UK's National Firefighter Selection Process
ISBN 978 0 7494 5161 5
How to Pass Verbal Reasoning Tests
ISBN 978 0 7494 5696 2
How to Succeed at an Assessment Centre
ISBN 978 0 7494 5688 7
IQ and Aptitude Tests
ISBN 978 0 7494 4931 5
IQ and Personality Tests
ISBN 978 0 7494 4954 4
IQ and Psychometric Tests
ISBN 978 0 7494 5106 6
IQ and Psychometric Test Workbook
ISBN 978 0 7494 4378 8
IQ Testing
ISBN 978 0 7494 5642 9
The Numeracy Test Workbook
ISBN 978 0 7494 4045 9
Preparing the Perfect Job Application
ISBN 978 0 7494 5653 5
Preparing the Perfect CV
ISBN 978 0 7494 5654 2
Readymade CVs
ISBN 978 0 7494 5323 7
Readymade Job Search Letters
ISBN 978 0 7494 5322 0
Succeed at IQ Tests
ISBN 978 0 7494 5228 5
Successful Interview Skills
ISBN 978 0 7494 5652 8
Test and Assess Your Brain Quotient
ISBN 978 0 7494 5416 6

Test and Assess Your IQ
ISBN 978 0 7494 5234 6
Test Your EQ
ISBN 978 0 7494 5535 4
Test Your IQ
ISBN 978 0 7494 5677 1
Test Your Numerical Aptitude
ISBN 978 0 7494 5064 9
Test Your Own Aptitude
ISBN 978 0 7494 3887 6
Ultimate Aptitude Tests
ISBN 978 0 7494 5267 4
Ultimate Cover Letters
ISBN 978 0 7494 5328 2
Ultimate CV
ISBN 978 0 7494 5327 5
Ultimate Interview
ISBN 978 0 7494 5387 9
Ultimate IQ Tests
ISBN 978 0 7494 5309 1
Ultimate Job Search
ISBN 978 0 7494 5388 6
Ultimate Psychometric Tests
ISBN 978 0 7494 5308 4
Verbal Reasoning Test Workbook
ISBN 978 0 7494 5150 9

Sign up to receive regular e-mail updates on Kogan Page books at **www.koganpage.com/signup.aspx** and visit our website: **www.koganpage.com**